Unit 6
Sales talk step-by-step

Unit 7
On the spot: dealing with special situations

Unit 8
After-sales

Focus on Communication

Grammar Hot Tips

Vocabulary

Bildquellen-verzeichnis

First Contacts

1

Content

STEP-IN – Your workplace

Task 1 What do you do?

a) *What can you say about your job? Draw a mind map about your job. Start like this:*

me and my job

- name + type of shop
- what it sells
- type of customers
- town/city
- who I work with
- what I like/don't like
- working hours
- my tasks

b) *Compare your mind map with a partner. Add more points where you can.*

Language tip

What do you do? = *Was ist Ihr Beruf?*
What are you doing? = *Was machen Sie gerade?*

Task 2 Everyday situations at work

a) *Describe the situations and the people in the photos. Say* **where** *they are,* **who** *they are,* **why** *they are there, and* **what** *they are saying.*

Useful language

to train as a sales assistant
to deal with customers
to have a job in retailing
to work at a branch of …
to be located in / near …
to be in charge of / responsible for …
to sell / make a sale
to buy/make a purchase
to work on / at the checkout / cash desk
to show / demonstrate …
to complain (about) …
to pay for the articles / goods
shop (BrE) / store (AmE)
department store
shopping centre (BrE)
shopping mall (AmE)

b) *Have you ever been in situations like these? As a customer or a sales assistant? Describe what happened.*

Task 3 Listening: Interview

a) *Listen to an interview with a trainee sales assistant. Note down what he says. Then compare your answers.*

b) *Listen again, and make a list of the journalist's questions. What else could he ask?*

Task 4 Talking shop

a) *Prepare a list of questions that you could use to interview people in your class. You can use ideas from your mind map and the listening practice.*

Language tip

Open questions help to start people talking:
What is ......
Where do you ......?
How long have you ......?
Closed questions usually produce a 'yes / no' response:
Do you ......? Is it ......? Did they ......?

Note

→ Find more about question forms in the Grammar Hot Tips section.

b) *Interview each other in pairs. Then compare your notes. What things do you have in common?*

Task 5 A personal profile

A personal profile is a useful basis for writing a CV (curriculum vitae, or résumé) or letter of application.

a) *Complete the missing words in this personal profile of Katja Bergmann.*

My name is Katja Bergmann. I am nineteen y............. old and I live in Grünwald, which is a sub................. of Munich.
I commute to work each day on the S-Bahn. I work as a trainee sales ass .... in Feldberger, a large d..................... store which is part of the Neu-Shopping Mall in the city centre.
This is my first job s..................... leaving school after my Abitur.

At the moment I am selling electrical equ.................... such as digital cameras, CD players and televisions. The work is interesting, and I like having co.............. with customers, but in the fu.................... I would like to work in the fashion department. I work four days a week in the store, and once a week I have classes at col.................... .
In my sp.................... time I like cooking Thai food, and at the weekends I go out on my motorbike if the w.................... is fine.

b) *Write a similar profile about yourself.*

As you gain more work experience, you can add more details to your profile.

Note

→ Find out more about writing for work in Focus on Communication.

STEP A – In the store

Task 1 Departments

a) *The items on p. 10 can usually be found in big department stores. Name them and match them with the departments on the in-store information board below.*

Example: Number 13 is a skateboard. You can find it in the Toys and Cycles department in the basement. Number 1 is a washing-machine. You can find it in the …

b) *What else can you buy in each department? Make notes.*

c) *What other departments might you find in a big department store? What would you find in them?*

d) *Customers often ask where they can find things in the store.*

Basement	**First Floor**
→ DIY	→ Ladies Fashion
→ Pets & Pet Foods	→ Sports & Leisure Clothing
→ Toys and Cycles	→ Textiles and Furnishings
Ground Floor	**Second Floor**
→ Furniture	→ Home Entertainment
→ Household Goods	→ Electrical Goods
→ Office Supplies	→ Sports Equipment

Excuse me, I'm looking for winter socks.

They're in the Sports and Leisure Clothing department.

Excuse me, where can I find films on DVD?

They're over there in the Home Entertainment section, next to the music CDs.

Work in pairs. Ask and answer where you can find things in the store. (Use your notes to help you.)

Task 2 A cup of coffee at the café

a) *Ask and answer questions with words from the boxes.*

Example:
- Where can I get a ***cup of coffee*** near here?
- You can get one ***at the café*** round the corner.

a	**cup** pair piece glass crate box loaf packet bottle tin kilo slice bar tube bag	**of**	cake shampoo beer chips beef earrings ham biscuits boots bread **coffee** butter oil tea cigarettes tights paint peas envelopes sweets toothpaste potatoes trousers matches chocolate	**from the** **at the**	stationer jeweller butcher bakery chemist **café** greengrocer shoe shop DIY store supermarket newsagents boutique vending machine pub

b) *The words above are all British English. Which ones mean the same as the American words below?*

can • candy • drugstore • jewelry store • French fries
pants • cookies • pantyhose

Task 3 Uncountable in English

a) *Complete the sentences with the words on the right.*

1. We bought some new .... for our living room.
2. You can find lots of useful .... in the brochures.
3. I've got some great .... for you. You've won € 500!
4. The waiter couldn't give us any .... about which wine to drink with our meal.
5. Could you give me some .... with these heavy boxes?

Language tip

No plural form
information, advice, experience, help, work, equipment, furniture, knowledge, news

b) *Make sentences with the other nouns.*

Note

→ Find more about uncountable nouns in the Grammar Hot Tips section.

Task 4 Sounds and spelling: Where's the stress?

a) *How do you say the word assistant? Is it <u>**ass**</u>istant, a<u>**ssis**</u>tant, or assist<u>**ant**</u>?*

b) *Copy the words on a piece of paper. Mark the syllable with the main stress, e.g. <u>re</u>tailing .*

c) *Listen and check.*

retailing • department • advice • understand • shampoo
checkout • sunglasses • expensive • success • colleague
furniture • equipment

Unit 1 First contacts

Task 5 Memory game

Play this game in groups.

Start like this …

The next person adds a word with 'b'.

And the next with 'c'.

Go on with the list – all the way to Z!

Task 6 Odd one out

Which word is the odd one out? Say why, and put the 'wrong' words in the 'right' group.

1. department store – **pens** – newsagent – boutique – butcher
2. apples – peaches – bananas – oranges – lego
3. envelopes – armchair – writing paper – pencils – glue
4. table – gloves – cupboard – sofa – bookcase
5. strawberries– doll – plastic gun – teddy bear – jigsaw
6. greengrocer – skirt – blouse – coat – jacket

Example: In the first group, 'pens' is the odd one out because the others are shops.

STEP B – Talking to customers

Task 1 Listening: Where are they?

Say where the people are, or where they are calling from.

souvenir shop • chemists • pet shop • toy shop • clothes shop
furniture shop • wine shop

Task 2 Quiz: Everyday English?

a) *Choose the best response.*

1. Excuse me, where are the teddy bears?
a) Teddy bears? Ask the manager. He knows.
b) I'm not sure. I'll just ask the manager.
c) Don't ask me. I'm new here.

2. I'm afraid I don't know how to do that.
a) Never mind, I'1ll show you.
b) I don't mind. You'll learn.
c) I don't care. That's your problem.

3. I'd like to speak to Mr Cooper, please.
a) Just one moment. I connect you.
b) Hold on a moment. I'm putting you through.
c) Wait a while, I'll call his extension number.

4. Hi, how are you?
a) Thanks, fine.
b) I am good.
c) Fine, thanks.

5. Excuse me, do you speak English?
a) Yes, of course.
b) Yes, I do. How can I help you?
c) Only a little.

6. Can I help you?
a) No, I'm just looking, thanks.
b) No, thanks. I only look.
c) No, leave me alone.

7. I'm afraid I've dropped a bottle of wine.
a) Oh, dear. That's terrible. You'll have to pay.
b) So what? It wasn't very good wine anyway.
c) Don't worry. I'll clear it up.

8. Can I pay in dollars?
a) No. You're in Europe, remember?
b) I'm afraid we only take euros.
c) Paying in dollars is not possible.

9. Do you accept credit cards?
a) Yes, of course.
b) Naturally.
c) Oh, all right.

10. Would you like a bag?
a) Thanks, no.
b) No, thanks.
c) Please, no.

11. Thanks very much for your help.
a) You're welcome.
b) Please.
c) Never mind.

12. Let me help you.
a) Leave me alone.
b) Thanks, you mustn't.
c) No, thanks, I can manage.

13. *(person sneezing)*
A-a-a-a-tishoo!
a) To your health!
b) Bless you!
c) Cheers!

14. Would you mind helping me with this?
a) Yes, of course.
b) Yes, I would mind.
c) No, not at all.

b) *Listen to the conversations again to check.*

Task 3 Customer service: Everyday expression

may • floor • right • I'd love one • I'm afraid • not at all
no, thanks • lift • can I offer you • would you mind • looking
please • here you are • excuse me • I'm sorry

a) *Complete the sentences with the missing expressions.*
1. *Sales assistant:* That's three euros, forty-five, (...).
Customer: Oh, dear. (...) I've only got a one hundred euro note.
Sales assistant: That's all (...), I can give you change.
2. *Customer:* (...), where are the toilets?
Sales assistant: They're on the first (...), opposite the (...).
3. *Customer:* (...) I speak to the manager, please?
Sales assistant: (...), but he's busy right now. (...) waiting a moment?
Customer: (...)
4. *Sales assistant:* Can I help you?
Customer: (...), I'm just (...).
5. *Sales assistant:* (...) a free glass of wine?
Customer: Yes, please, (...)!
Sales assistant: (...) It's a dry Riesling. What do you think?

b) *Listen and check.*

Task 4 What are they saying?

a) *Work in groups of three. Write the dialogue between the customer and the sales assistant in the story on the next page. Use the 'everyday English' expressions you have learned.*

b) *Act out your dialogue to the class.*

Task 5 Giving directions in the store

BE: lift
AE: elevator

Excuse me, where can I find men's shirts

Take the lift to the second floor. Then turn right and the Menswear section is straight ahead.

I'm looking for candles. Do you sell them here?

Yes, we do sell candles. You'll find them in Home Furnishings in the basement, next to the Garden Centre.

Useful language

to turn left • to turn right • to go straight on • to keep going • to go up to the next floor • to go downstairs • to take the lift • opposite the cash desk • at the top of the escalator • in the food hall • next to the gift shop • on the kitchen display • above the frying pans • beneath the Special Offer sign • on the last shelf on the right • near the restaurant • in front of the main entrance • behind the pillar

The diagram below shows the layout of the ground floor of a department store.

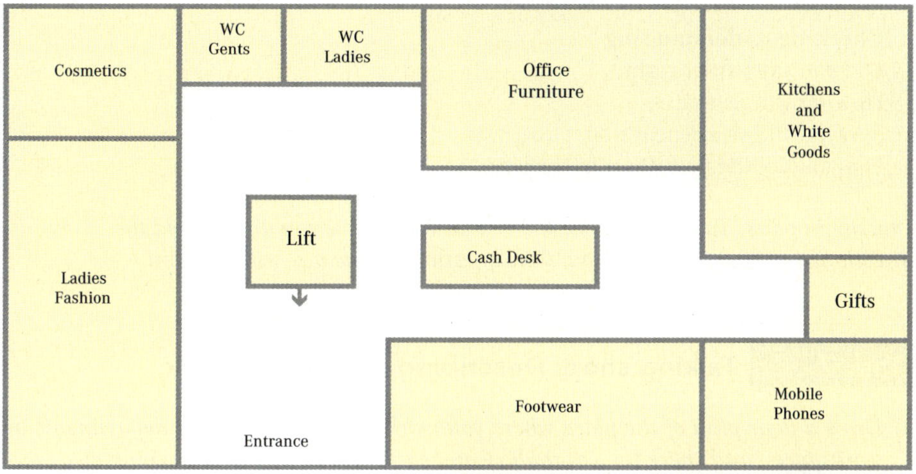

a) *A sales assistant on the second floor tells a customer where to find dishwashers.*
Complete the missing words in her directions.

We have a wide ra.................... of dishwashers in the White Goods department on the gr.................. floor.

T.................... the lift and then turn.................... and go s.................... on, past the c.................... ...., and you will see the White Goods on the left, n.................... to the ....

The dishwashers are at the back, in b.................... the freezers and the washing-machines.

b) *Work in pairs. First decide where you are in the store, and then take it in turns to be the customer. Ask for directions to goods or services that would be located on the ground floor.*

Task 6 A visitor to your college

How would you give directions in English to a visitor to your college?
The visitor might be looking for:

- The secretary's office.
- The way back to the car park.
- The nearest photocopier machine.
- The staff room
- ...... ?

Useful language

Checking understanding
Did you say left, or right?
How far is it, exactly?
Sorry, could you repeat that, please?
Did you say the first door on the left?

Practise in pairs. Take turns to be the visitor. Make sure you understand the directions your partner gives you. (The questions in the box will help you.)

Task 7 Talking shop: Describing where you work

a) *Draw a floor plan of the place where you work. Label the different departments or workspaces, and check the vocabulary and spelling. When you have completed your plan on paper, make a PowerPoint presentation.*

b) *Give a short presentation to your group. Talk about where you work, the layout of the shop, what it sells and what you do.*

Language tip

- Introduce yourself and your topic clearly.
- Divide your talk into two or three separate parts.
- Sum up the key points at the end.
- Finish by asking the audience if they have any questions.
- Try not to read from notes, but use prompt cards with key information.

LEARNING SKILLS – Starting a language file

As you go through this book, you will find lots of tips for learning English. A good first step is to start a personal language file with sections for organising your material. It will help you to find things, and to revise for tests and exams.

Name: __________

English for Sales Assistants

Vocabulary
- Alphabetical word list
- Retail outlets
- Products and services
- Exercises

Grammar
- Tips and rules
- Exercises

Communication
- Telephoning
- Talking with customers
- Writing for work

Tests

Homework

Notes

Task 1 Organising the file

The personal language file above has dividers for each section.

a) *Can you add any more sections?*

b) *Decide on the best order for the sections in your file.*

Task 2 What goes where?

Say where you would put these pieces of paper in your file.

1
Types of company
greengrocer
butcher
chemist
supermarket
bakery

2
Name: Jan Maier **Date:** 8th June
Test No. 3
A Vocabulary
Give the opposites.
1. expesive: cheap ✓

3
Put in 'some' *or* 'any'.
1. Have you got *any* change?
2. I'd like *some* information, please.
3. There aren't *any* boxes left.
4. *Some* customers have just arrived.
5. Would you like *some* more tea?

4 Present progressive
– I **am wearing** jeans.
(at the moment)

Simple present
– I **wear** jeans.
(sometimes / often / always)

5 *Dear Mr Granger,*
Thank you for your enquiry of 6th May in which you asked about the price of our new ABC model.
Please find enclosed our current price list as well as details of payment and delivery.
We look forward to receiving your order.
Yours sincerely,

6 Useful phrases
Assistant: Can I help you?
Customer: No, I'm just looking, thanks.
Customer: Excuse me, where do I pay for these?
Assistant: Over at the cash desk.

7 after-sales: *Kundendienst*
apprentice: *Lehrling*
apprenticeship: *Lehre*
branch: *Filiale, Zweigstelle*
brand: *Markenname*

8 Class trip: 23rd May

9 He-she-it, 's' muss mit.
If + would = Satz kaputt

As you go through this unit, remember to file things away in your language file.

In Unit 2 you will find some tips on how to record vocabulary.

WORD POWER

Task 1 Nouns and verbs

a) *Match the verbs on the left with the nouns on the right.*

unpack tidy help phone send put price tags on stack work	the shelves at the checkout / the cash desk the shop customers emails suppliers the goods the delivery

b) *Work in pairs. Ask and answer questions about each other's everyday tasks.*

Example: Do you ever work at the cash desk? Yes, I do, but only when we're very busy.

Task 2 'a pair of'

a) *Match what the customer says with the sales assistant's answers.*

1. The jeans fit, but they're a bit too short.
2. These shorts are much too big for me.
3. These nail scissors are very expensive.
4. Do you think these sunglasses suit me? → e)
5. Sorry, but I've broken this pair of scales.

a) *Would you like to try on a smaller pair?*
b) *Well, I'm afraid you'll have to pay for them.*
c) *This pair is a bit cheaper, but good quality.*
d) *I'm sorry, but we haven't got a longer pair.*
e) *Yes, they look great on you!*

b) *What other answers can the sales assistant give? Make dialogues with a partner.*

Task 3 Prepositions

Put in the missing prepositions.

with • about • in • for • of

1. Who is responsible .... cleaning the toilets?
2. You can pay .... the articles at the checkout.
3. I want to complain .... the bad service.
4. Sometimes sales assistants have to deal .... difficult customers.
5. Mr Rogers is .... charge .... the sales department.
6. Someone asked .... a pair .... size 52 black tights!

Learning tip

Note down new words with the prepositions they go with.

Products and Services

2

Content

STEP-IN – Bestsellers

Task 1 Sales talk: Describing products

impractical • ugly • up-to-date • convenient • well-made
inexpensive • badly-designed • useful • stylish • faulty
disappointing • versatile • overpriced • old-fashioned
unreliable • attractive • efficient • healthy

Check the meaning of the words above. Which ones could you use to sell the products where you work? Which would you never use in selling?

Task 2 Listening: Window-shopping

Two people are looking into a shop window. *Listen and note down:*

- the three products they talk about
- the good and bad points of each one.

Task 3 Famous brands

Work in pairs. Choose one of the brands below but don't give the name of the brand. Describe it to your partner. Can s/he guess which one it is?

Example You can find the stores in most towns and cities.
They offer the latest fashion for women, men and children.

Useful language

Price
to offer (excellent) value for money
to be reasonably priced
to sell at a competitive price

Reputation and quality
to be of superior quality
to have a (good) reputation for …
to stand for quality
to be the market leader in …

Style and fashion
to be stylish / fashionable/trendy
to be traditional / classic
to have an attractive design
to be 'in'/to be 'the latest in …'

Technology and use
to be (highly) sophisticated
to be state-of-the-art
to be well-made / -built / -constructed
to be reliable / robust / durable
to be efficient / economical
to be user-friendly / easy-to-use
to be versatile / to have many uses
to offer convenience / comfort
to be convenient / useful / handy
to be comfortable

Task 4 Talking shop: Bestsellers

a) *Make a list of the best-selling brands or product lines in your shop. Explain why they are so successful.*

A product that always sells well is …

At the moment our best-selling brand is …

Language tip

- **product range:** products belonging to different categories
- **product line:** group of products belonging to one category, with the same brand name

b) *Have there been any flops? What was the reason?*

Task 5 Talking point: No-name brands

Do you buy (or sell) no-name brands? Talk about their advantages and disadvantages.

On the one hand, ...	On the other hand, ...	No-name brands are …,	whereas brands ...

STEP A – The Christmas flyer

The big Frankfurt department store *Morath* has produced a four-page flyer in English to attract foreign visitors to do their Christmas shopping in the store.

MORATH
Christmas Gifts for her

Thai silk scarves
Lovely colours and the finest quality

Crystal glass cats
Delicate glassware, many types of cats

Bath and body collection
Natural fragrances and famous brands

Aztec jewellery
Authentic items from Mexico

Suede gloves and handbags
Soft leather in a range of colours

Bring this flyer along for a free glass of mulled wine!

MORATH
Christmas Feast

Spicy Christmas biscuits
A traditional Christmas favourite

Marzipan fruit
Colourful and delicious speciality

Five fine wines
A French and Italian selection

Basket of exotic nuts
Nuts from around the world

Belgian truffles
Fine black and white chocolate

MORATH
Christmas Gifts for him

Wireless pocket organiser
The ultimate executive accessory

Cosmetics for men
Presented in a luxury leather case

Stainless-steel diver's watch
Guaranteed waterproof to 200m

Cordless power drill
With a range of attachments

Carved wooden chess set
Hand-made by craftsmen in Sweden

MORATH
Kids' Stuff

Grizzly bear
With rough fur and a big growl

Hot air balloon
Model balloon complete with gas burner

Circus unicycle
With easy-to-follow instructions

Master Blaster
New video game for space travellers

Enamelling kit
Make your own badges and earrings

Task 1 Quiz

a) *Find words in the flyer for the following things:*

1. Six items that people wear.
2. Two items that people carry things in.
3. Words that mean the same as these:

scents • cookies • genuine
simple • astronauts • tasty

4. Words that mean the opposite of these:

artificial • smooth • unknown
out-of-date • tough

Language tip

wear/worn/worn
I always **wear** glasses for reading.
carry/carried/carry
I never **carry** heavy bags.

b) 'Nationality' *words. (Make a grid like the one on the right.)*

c) *You have received these postcards from friends on holiday. Where are they? What adjective would you use for each country?*

noun	adjective
Spain	Spanish
Switzerland	Swiss
Holland	Dutch
. . .	. . .

Task 2 Sales talk: Helping customers choose

A customer comes into the Morath department store to do some Christmas shopping. She asks the sales assistant for help.

Excuse me, I'm looking for a present for my sister. I want to give her something unusual.

Does she like jewellery? We have some lovely silver from Mexico

That sounds interesting. May I have a look at it?

Certainly. Would you like to follow me, please?

a) *In pairs, take it in turns to be the customer and the assistant. The assistant helps the customer to find a suitable present from the flyer for these people:*

a ten-year-old girl
a twenty-year-old student
a sixty-year-old grandad

b) *Now try to choose a present for a friend or family member. This time, the sales assistant can also suggest items from other departments in the store.*

Useful language

I'm looking for …
I'm trying to find …
I'd like to buy …
Follow me, please.
We've got a nice …
Or if you prefer …
I'd suggest …
That sounds interesting …
What is it, exactly?
That's rather expensive.
It's top quality.

STEP B – Choosing a cuckoo-clock

Petra, a sales assistant in a Munich souvenir shop, is talking to an American tourist.

Petra: Are you being served, madam?
Customer: No, not yet. I've been trying to find someone to help me!
Petra: I'm sorry – the Oktoberfest is our busiest time of year. What can I do for you?
Customer: I'm looking for gifts for the folks back home – something typically German.
Petra: Well, you've come to the best place! Are you interested in anything in particular?
Customer: Maybe one of those Swiss cuckoo-clocks. There are so many different kinds!
Petra: Actually, cuckoo-clocks originated in Germany. They're one of our most popular gifts.
Customer: There's an amazing one over there. It's the biggest I've ever seen!
Petra: That's the 'Jäger'. Would you like to listen to it?

Customer: Yes, I'd love to … But I'd really prefer something smaller and less expensive.

Petra: Have a look at these. They're our tiniest clocks, so they're ideal as small gifts.

Customer: I can see they're the cheapest, too, but they're plastic. I want something made of wood, and more interesting.

Petra: Let me show you this one. It's a genuine hand-carved clock from the Black Forest town of Triberg, and it's not as expensive as the bigger clocks.

Customer: Oh, that's much better, and I love the carvings. Leaves are so much nicer than hunting guns. It has a prettier sound, too.

Petra: What about this one? It's similar, but the wood is a lighter colour. It's a bit cheaper, too.

Customer: Actually, I prefer the darker one. On the other hand, it's more expensive, so I don't know which one to buy. It's so hard to decide, so … I'll take both! Do you ship to the States?

Petra: Yes, we do. Where are you from?

Customer: Illinois – do you know it?

Petra: I've haven't been there, but I know it's very different from the Black Forest – and a lot flatter!

'Titisee' €5.99

'Schönwald' €45.99

'Triberg' €49.99

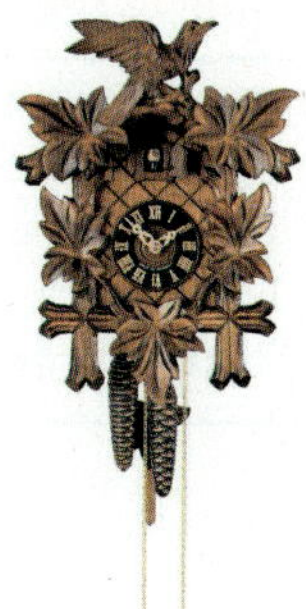

'Jäger' €299

Task 1 Comparing clocks

a) *Four of the sentences are false. Correct the mistakes.*

1. The busiest time of year for the souvenir shop is Christmas.
2. The 'Titisee' is the tiniest clock and it's also the cheapest.
3. The 'Schönwald' is lighter than the 'Triberg', and it is five euros cheaper.
4. The 'Triberg' is more expensive than the 'Schönwald', but cheaper than the 'Jäger'.
5. The customer thinks that the 'Triberg' has a prettier sound than the 'Jäger'.
6. The 'Jäger' is the most expensive clock, and it has the lightest wood.
7. The customer tells Petra that Illinois is much flatter than Bavaria.

b) *Which cuckoo-clock (or clocks) does the customer decide to buy? Explain why.*

Task 2 Shop talk

Work in groups. Find out what your shops have in common and what is different, and make comparisons.

Example Tanja's shop is **bigger than** Kai's.
My shop is **the most expensive.**
Shoes at Mario's shop are **not as cheap as** where Sarah works.

Language tip

(not) **as** cheap **as**
(not) **as** expensive **as**
cheaper **than**
more expensive **than**
the cheapest
the most expensive

Note

→ Find more about comparative forms in the Grammar Hot Tips section.

Task 3 Describing products and uses

a) *Put the words in the right groups. Some can go in more than one group. Add more words that are useful to you.*

glass ~~sapphire~~ striped green
~~aluminium~~ silver wool gold
emerald cotton blue plastic
iron diamond lead ~~check~~
suede turquoise polka dot ~~lace~~

Metals	Fabrics and fibres
• *gold* • …	• *lace* • …
Materials	**Patterns**
• *aluminium* • …	• *check* • …
Gems	**Colours**
• *sapphire* • …	• … • …

b) *A salesman is presenting a new product to a retailer of electronic goods.*

'Our new telephone simulator is a piece of equipment that is used by call centres and language schools for training telephone skills. It's small and portable, and it's made of a new type of plastic so it's very light. In fact, it weighs less than 500 grams. It consists of two phone handsets that are attached to a device that records the conversations. Afterwards, you can play back the recordings and listen to the speakers. The great thing is that it uses blue-tooth technology, which means that there are no cables or wires. Because of this, it's very easy to assemble.'

Have you heard of a product like this? Discuss whether it would sell well in Germany, and who would buy it.

c) *Describe a product that you know well, and ask other people in your class to guess what it is.*

Useful language

It is used by …
It is a thing / device / tool / piece of equipment for …
It is used for (+ -ing verb)/to (+ infinitive)
It is tiny / small / medium-sized / large …
It is made of / consists of …
It works like this. You …
The great thing is that …, which means …
Because of this, it's …

Task 4 Sales talk

a) *'Are you being served' is a useful phrase for sales assistants. Complete the gaps in the phrases below with the help of the dialogue on page 21.*

1. What can I … for you?
2. Are you interested in anything in p…?
3. … you like to listen to it?
4. Have a l… at these.
5. Let me s… you this one.
6. What … this one?

b) *Work in pairs or groups. First, make a list of products you would like to sell. Decide who will be the sales assistants and the customers. Practise describing your products, using the language you have learned so far.*

STEP C – Announcements

Task 1 Sounds and spelling: Minimal pairs

a) *Listen and say which words you hear.*

1.	a) a sheep pen	b) a cheap pen	6.	a) I work a lot.	b) I walk a lot.
2.	a) a new pan	b) a new pen	7.	a) invite	b) in white
3.	a) a pig pen	b) a big pen	8.	a) forty kids	b) four tickets
4.	a) a long ship	b) a long chip	9.	a) I'm sinking.	b) I'm thinking.
5.	a) a hot egg	b) a hard egg	10.	a) hairy shoulder	b) Harry's older

b) *Choose any ten words from the list below. Write them down and then dictate them to someone else. Then check the answers. (If there are no mistakes, you have pronounced the words clearly!)*

bad – bed • had – head • wet – vet • sale – sell • man – men
thing – sing • all white – all right • chip – ship
marry – Mary – merry • ferry – very • hard – heart • head – hot
pair – pear • bear – beer

Task 2 Listening: In-store announcements

Listen to the announcements and answer the questions.

Part 1

1. Which departments do the announcements mention? Where can you find them?
2. Name four things you can buy in each department.
3. Which department has a sale at the moment?
4. Which department is very new?
5. What can you get for only €29.99?

Part 2

1. What has been found, and what does it look like?
2. Where was it found?
3. Where is it now?

Task 3 Writing for work

a) *Work in groups of three. Write in-store announcements for the following products*

Useful phrases

Come and see ...
We have everything you're looking for!
There's something for everyone.
You can choose from ...
Browse in our ...
Browse through our range of ...
Compare ...
You'll find plenty to interest you ...
You'll also find an amazing selection of ...
We have special offers all this week.
New saucepans for only €9.99!
Everything is on sale.
All our prices are reduced.
Our staff will be happy to advise you.
Don't miss this great opportunity!

b) *Read your announcements to other people in your class. Decide who has the best announcements.*

STEP D – How things work

Task 1 Listening: Assembling a Christmas pyramid

a) *Put the pictures in the right order. Then listen to the recording and check your answers.*

A

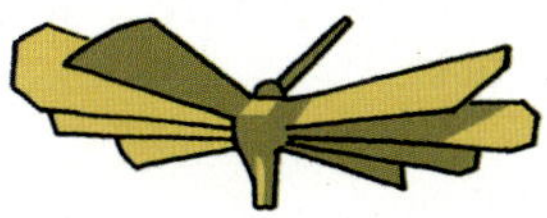

The heat turns the propeller.

B

Stand the base on the table.

C

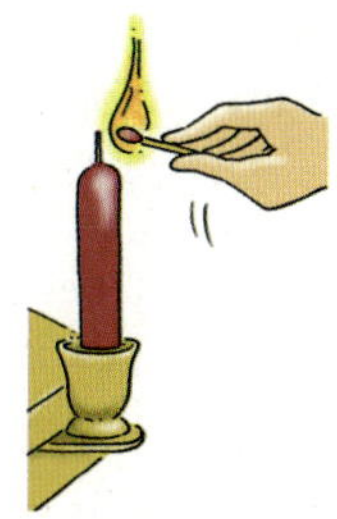

Light the candle in the base.

D

After that, put the angels on the outside.

E

The angels rotate and strike bells with a hammer.

F

Then fit the central part to make a shape like a pyramid.

b) *How long does the pyramid turn, and what does the assistant say about small children? Listen again if you need to.*

Task 2 Sales talk: How does work?

Read or listen to the dialogues and answer the questions on the next page.

Dialogue 1

Customer: Can you tell me about this machine, please? It looks very stylish, but is it complicated to use?

Assistant: No, not at all, it's very user-friendly. Would you like a demonstration?

Customer: Yes, please.

Assistant: Well, the first step is to fill this tank with cold water. The container on the other side is for the beans. Then simply plug in the machine and switch it on. Do you see the little red light?

Customer: Yes. Does that mean it's ready?

Assistant: No, not yet. It's warming up. But it only takes sixty seconds. And you can also set the machine for the size of cup you want. Have a go!

Customer: Okay. Now the red light has turned green. Can I press the button?

Assistant: Yes, please go ahead.

Customer: Wow, that's fast, and not too noisy. Does it come with a guarantee?

Dialogue 2

Customer: Excuse me. I want to buy one of these for my daughter, but I've never used one myself. Could you show me how it works?

Assistant: Of course, madam. The first thing to remember is to put the strap round your wrist, like this, so that you can't drop it. Then press this button to switch on.

Customer: Oh, yes. The little screen lights up.

Assistant: You can switch the screen off if you want to save battery life. Then you have a zoom button on top, and the shutter to take the picture. You can store up to fifty pictures on the memory stick.

Customer: Does it come with a battery?

Assistant: Yes, if I press here the battery pops out. There it is.

Customer: I've never seen one like that before.

1. What products are they talking about? Say how you know.
2. For each product, think of other questions that the customer might ask.
3. What question might the assistant ask?

Task 3 Writing for work

a) *Choose one of the items below. Find out how it works. Write a description for an instruction booklet.*

b) *Choose a product from your store. If possible, bring it to class and demonstrate how to use ist.*

LEARNING SKILLS – Taking vocabulary notes

Task 1 Organising words

Match the tips with the vocabulary notes below. (Sometimes there is more than one right answer.)

A Explain words in English.
B Write the word in a sentence to show how it is used.
C Put the words in groups or categories.
D Put the words in alphabetical order.
E Translate the word into your own language.
F Show the meaning with an opposite.
G Add partner verbs/prepositions, e. g. to **do** homework, to look **up** a word
H Write down the word in its different forms.

1 *Skiing equipment: poles – skis – boots – goggles – gloves*

4 *knife (sing.)*
knives (pl.)

2 *competition (n.)*
competitor (n.)
to compete with (v.)
competitive (adj.)

5 *economical – money-saving*
An economical car is cheap to run.
Opposite: wasteful

6 *sell – sold – sold*
to be sold out
to sell like hot cakes

3 *queue – a line of people waiting*
There's a long queue of customers at the checkout.
to queue (up) for something – to wait in a line

7 *to complain about a product*
to do an apprenticeship

8 *after-sales: Kundendienst*
appointment: Termin
apprentice: Lehre

Task 2 Word groups

a) *Put the words in groups.*

b) *Add two words to each list.*

wear with polite up umbrella under ~~buy~~ helpful sale remember write supervisor through wait friendly cup

nouns	verbs
	• *buy*
prepositions	**adjectives**

Task 3 Verb-noun partners

a) *What is the simple past form of these verbs?*
b) *Use the verbs to complete the text*

spend • go • make
do • have

Susanne (....................) a day off from work yesterday. She (....................) shopping in London and she (....................) a great time. First she (.................) on the London Eye, and then she bought some new clothes. In fact, she (.............) most of her money in Harrods. In the evening she (....................) a wonderful meal. She (....................) the cooking, and her boyfriend (....................) the washing up. Later, they (....................) for a walk together in the rain. The following day, Susanne (....................) a bad cold. She (....................) a quick phone call to her boss, and then she (....................) the rest of the day in bed.

Task 4 Explaining words

How can you explain the words on the right? Discuss the best way to record them in your vocabulary book.

light bulb • dirty • delicious
jewellery • to promise
expensive • to advise

WORD POWER

Task 1 Matching words

a) *Sort the products into categories. Suggest further examples to add to each group.*
b) *Name some popular brands for each category. Do you buy them? Why, or why not?*

Cosmetics • Tableware • Furniture • Kitchen appliances
Detergents • Stationery • Sports equipment

envelope • tennis racket • chest of drawers • mascara • dinner plate
washing-up liquid • toaster • pen • cup • lipstick • microwave
ski poles • glue • bed • fabric softener • dessert bowl • eyeliner
kettle • football • note paper

Task 2 English words in Germany

a) *You often see and hear English in Germany – on signs and notices, or in advertisements.*

Make the most of now.

Postbank

Can you think of more examples? Why do you think English words are used in Germany?

b) *Here are some German words that English-speakers use.*

rucksack • kindergarten • schnapps • lederhosen • autobahn
kitsch • kaput[1] *• muesli*

How would you explain them in English to a customer who isn't from an English-speaking country?

Task 3 How things work

Complete the sales demonstration with the missing words. (There are more words than gaps!)

press • ready • takes • plug it in • store • light up • put in
complicated • remove • switch it on • replace • easy to use
warm up • finished • turn it off • select • pull • save • cool down

This new photocopier is very .... The first thing to do is .... and then .... It .... about five minutes to .... When it is ...., a green button will .... Simply .... the number of copies you want and .... the 'ON' button. If there's a paper jam, you don't need to .... The machine will show you exactly where the problem is. Just .... the paper and the photocopier will function properly again. It is easy to .... the printer cartridge. Just take out the old one and .... the new one.

Task 4 What does it come with?

a) *Say what each item comes with.*

Example: The jacket comes with one spare button.

1 *Im Deutschen: kaputt*

1.  + 

2.  + 

3.  + 

4.  + 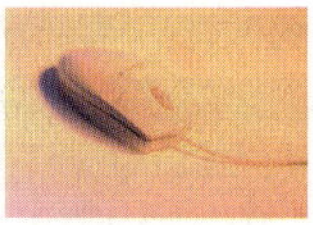

5.  + 

b) *Talk about the products you sell. What do they come with?*

CHECK-OUT 1

A Questions

Here are Katja's answers in an interview. Write the interview with the reporter's questions.

Example ***Reporter:*** What is your name?
Katja: My name is Katja Bergmann.

1. My name is Katja Bergmann.
2. I'm a sales assistant.
3. I live in Grünwald.
4. In a department store called Feldberger.
5. Yes, it's my first job.
6. I've been working there for six months.
7. No, I only work four days a week.
8. At 9 o'clock in the morning, which isn't too early.
9. Yes, I do. I have them once a week at college.
10. Because I like my colleagues and I meet so many interesting people.

What …?
Where …?
When …?
Why …?
Is it …?
How long …?
Do you …?

B Prepositions

Complete the sentences with the words, and add the missing prepositions. Be careful with the verb form.

pay • consist • come • make • ~~complain~~ • deal • responsible

1. If you're unhappy with the service, you should **complain about** it.
2. In my job I have to … many different kinds of customers.
3. Mrs Bauer is … all the trainees in my shop.

4. Customers ... their shopping at the checkout or cash desk.
5. The stationery kit ... a folder, some writing paper, envelopes and a beautiful pen.
6. The folder ... leather.
7. Does the toy ... batteries?

C Everyday English

Match the statements/questions with the responses.

1. Hi, how are you? → f)
2. Can I help you?
3. Would you like a bag?
4. Can I pay by credit card?
5. Thanks for your help.
6. Would you mind if I used your phone?
7. Have you got any change?

a) *Yes, of course.*
b) *No, thanks. I'm just looking.*
c) *I'm afraid not.*
d) *You're welcome.*
e) *No, not at all.*
f) *I'm fine, thanks*
g) *Yes, please.*

1 CHECK-OUT

D Departments

List five things you can buy in each department.

1. Pets
2. Furniture
3. Ladies' Fashion
4. Office Supplies
5. Sports Equipment
6. Toys

Ladies' Fashion

E Different words, same meaning

Say it in a different way. Choose from the words in the box.

1. Our CD players are very **easy to use**.
2. Those shoes are really **'in'** at the moment.
3. I prefer a **classic** design.
4. These saucepans are **good value for money**.
5. This kitchen 'Magimix' **has many uses**.
6. I love post-it notes. They're so **handy**.
7. This brand **has an excellent reputation** for quality.

very versatile
convenient
stands
traditional
user-friendly
very reasonably priced
fashionable

F Opposites

Give the opposites of the words that are marked

I bought a **large** teddy bear with **rough** fur that was **factory**-made in Germany. It's an **unknown** brand, and it was quite **cheap**.

G Grammar

Choose the correct option.

1. Could you give me (some / an / a) advice about the wine?
2. I always (wear / carry) glasses for reading.
3. It's a very (economic / economical) car.
4. I'm (making / doing) an apprenticeship.
5. At the moment I (work / am working) in a shoe shop.
6. I think that French is (more hard than / harder than / harder as) English.
7. I don't think English is (so difficult as / as difficult as) Chinese.

H Translation

a) *Translate into English.*
1. Die Hose steht Ihnen sehr gut.
2. Ich hätte gern vier Scheiben Schinken.
3. Tragen Sie eine Brille?
4. Das Gerät braucht fünf Minuten um aufzuwärmen.

b) *Translate into German.*
1. May I have a look at those watches?
2. I'm just looking, thanks.
3. I'm looking for a gift for my sister.
4. It's my day off tomorrow.
5. Everything is on sale.

I British or American English?

a) *Is the speaker using British or American English?*
1. I'd like some fries with my burger.
2. Excuse me, where can I find ladies' tights?
3. German biscuits are absolutely delicious!
4. Is it possible to buy candy in a German drugstore?

b) *Give the British / American alternatives.*

Customers

3

Content
STEP-IN – Shopping habits
STEP A – Telephone enquiries
STEP B – Everyday English
STEP C – Written communication
LEARNING SKILLS – Learning Vocabulary
WORD POWER

STEP-IN – Shopping habits

Task 1 Talking shop: Quiz

a) *Try this quiz and then compare your answers with a partner. Explain your choices.*

1. *I prefer to go shopping ...*
   a) alone.
   b) with one or two friends.
   c) in a group.
2. *Choosing a new pair of jeans takes me ...*
   a) less than fifteen minutes.
   b) between fifteen minutes and an hour.
   c) longer than an hour.
3. *I expect sales assistants to ...*
   a) leave me alone to make up my own mind.
   b) be very polite and give me lots of attention.
   c) treat me like one of their friends.
4. *When I'm shopping for clothes, I ...*
   a) try to spend as little as possible.
   b) always stay within my budget.
   c) often overspend if I see something I like.

5. *When I'm buying shampoo, I ...*
   a) often try new brands out of curiosity.
   b) only try new brands recommended by friends.
   c) always choose the same brand.

6. *On my way to meet a friend, I notice that my favourite shop is having a sale. I ...*
   a) pop inside quickly to get the best bargains.
   b) decide to go back the next day.
   c) meet my friend and we go to the sale together.

7. *When I buy clothes for a party, they last ...*
   a) long enough to wear at lots more parties.
   b) until the first washing.
   c) Who cares? I never wear the same outfit twice.

8. *When I'm choosing new trainers, the three most important things I look for are ...*
   a) low price
   b) the brand
   c) simple design
   d) special features
   e) comfort
   f) being different from everyone else

9. *I usually wear clothes made of ...*
   a) natural fibres, such as cotton, silk or wool.
   b) synthetic fibres, such as nylon or polyester.
   c) whatever is in fashion.

b) *Read the article and decide what type of customer your partner is like. Find out, if he / she agrees.*

What type of customer are you?	
The individualist:	You know exactly what you want. Sometimes you want to browse, but you don't like being pestered by sales assistants.
The impulse-buyer:	You often buy things on a whim, usually things you don't need.
The 'me-too' shopper:	You want to be like your friends, and have what they have. Advertising also has a strong influence on you.
The price-shopper:	You always keep an eye open for bargains. You read the price tags, and look for discounts and special offers. Getting the best deal is important to you.
The snob-shopper:	You are very status-conscious. You want people to admire you, and you buy only the most exclusive brands.
The green shopper:	You always buy organic food and products made of natural materials. You avoid products that are bad for the environment or that have been tested on animals.
The chatterbox:	You like sales assistants who are interested in you and have time to talk to you.
The sceptic:	You don't like taking risks. You compare products and check them carefully before buying them. You also ask lots of questions.
The ditherer:	You find it hard to decide, and often leave shops without buying anything.
The magpie:	You get bored easily, and you love trying out new brands and products.

Task 2 Customer talk

Which of the types of customer in the article on page 40 might say these things?

I'm just looking, thanks. • *I'm not sure – I'll think about it.*
Is the price reduced on this? • *I'd prefer recycled paper, please.*
Does this toaster come with a guarantee?

Task 3 Listening: Finding out what customers want

a) *You are going to hear three conversations.*
As you listen, note down:
- where the customers are,
- what they want to do, or buy,
- what each sales assistant offers or suggests.

b) *Compare the assistants. Do they make any mistakes? What tips would you give them?*

c) *Read the list of phrases on the right. Listen again and say which ones you hear.*

Learning tip

Good morning / afternoon.
Can I help you (at all)?
Would you like some help?
Are you looking for anything in particular?
Would you like me to show you …?
Perhaps you're interested in …
What do you need it for?
Would you like to look at …?
Have you got anything in mind?
How / What about …?
If you need any help, just let me know.
If I can help in any way, just ask.

Task 4 Expressions with 'mind'

a) *Match the English sentences with the German translations.*

1. What sort of price do you have in **mind**?	a) *Vorsicht, Stufe!*
2. I don't **mind**.	b) *Ich kann mich nicht entscheiden.*
3. Have you got anything special in **mind**?	c) *Es ist mir egal.*
4. I can't make my **mind** up.	d) *Was ist Ihre Preisvorstellung?*
5. **Mind** the step!	e) *Denken Sie an etwas besonderes?*
6. Never **mind**.	f) *Macht nichts.*

b) *Here are some more expressions with 'mind'. How would you translate them?*

1. I've got no idea. My **mind's a** complete **blank**!
2. I'm **in two minds** about buying the flat.
3. I can't **get** that song **out of my mind**.
4. I usually remember her birthday, but this year it just **slipped my mind**.
5. I've **changed my mind**. I think I'll buy it after all.
6. I'd go **out of my mind** if I had to stack shelves all day.
7. **If you don't mind my asking**, how much do you earn a month?
8. **Mind your own business!**
9. **Bear in mind** that many of our customers are pensioners.

Task 5 Talking shop

Talk about the type of customers who come into your shop. Have you got any tips on dealing with them?

STEP A – Telephone enquiries

Task 1 A phone call to ComputerWorld

a) *Read or listen to the dialogue and answer the questions.*

Assistant: ComputerWorld, Brenner, guten Tag.
Customer: Oh, good morning. Do you speak English?
Assistant: Yes, no problem. How can I help you?
Customer: I have an Apple computer and I need a new mouse.
Assistant: I see. Could you tell me which model of computer it is?
Customer: It's an iMac, I bought it about two years ago.
Assistant: And is there a problem with the mouse?
Customer: No, but I'd prefer an infra-red one so that I don't have the cable on the desk.
Assistant: Yes, the infra-red ones are more convenient, but I'm afraid we don't have any in stock at the moment. There's been so much demand for them. Would you like me to order one for you?
Customer: Oh dear. How long would that take?
Assistant: It normally takes about three working days, so it could be here by Friday.
Customer: Oh, that's great! That means I can pick it up at the weekend. I thought it would take weeks.
Assistant: If you give me your name and phone number, I'll call you when it arrives.
Customer: Yes, my name is James Burke, that's B-U-R-K-E, and my number is 0721 – that's the area code – and then it's 378 374. Have you got that?
Assistant: Yes, Mr Burke. I'll just read it back to you. It's 0721 378 374.
Customer: Exactly. Oh, by the way, could you tell me how much it costs? I forgot to ask!
Assistant: I'll just check for you … Ah, here it is. Yes, it's on special offer, at only €45.99.
Customer: Brilliant! Anyway, I look forward to hearing from you on Friday. Goodbye.
Assistant: Bye.

1. Why does the customer want to buy an infra-red mouse?
2. How long does it normally take to order one?
3. The customer nearly forgets to ask a very important question. What is it?
4. When will the customer speak to the sales assistant again?

b) *Put in the prepositions. Then complete the summary of the phone call with the expressions.*

1. ...... special offer
2. ...... demand
3. ...... the weekend
4. ...... stock
5. ...... Friday (at the latest)
6. ...... the moment

Summary of customer enquiry
The customer wanted to buy an infra-red mouse, but I told him that we don't have any infra-red models .... because they are really .... them .... I offered to order one, and when I promised it would be in the shop ...., he decided to buy one and said he would pick it up .... He was also very pleased that it's ....

Unit 3 Customers

Language tip

A **wireless** mouse has no **cable**.

Task 2 Confirming details

a) *Put the parts of this phone call in the right order.*

A Customer: Good, and we decided that the floral displays for the conference room are red and the ones in the lobby are blue. Is that clear?
B Assistant: Not at all. It's good to double-check the details. I wish you every success with your event.
C Customer: Could you also supply us with three small bouquets with a mixture of red and blue flowers?
D Assistant: Good morning, Mrs Knowles. This is Katja Jorgensen. It's nice to speak to you again.

E Assistant: Floribunda, guten Tag. ← ***Start here***

F Customer: You see, those are the colours of the new brands we're launching at the conference.
G Assistant: Goodbye Mrs Knowles.
H Customer: Hello, this is Mrs Knowles from KK Consulting.
I Assistant: Don't worry, Mrs Knowles, we're used to doing this kind of display. And at the end of the conference, we'll come and take the flowers away.
J Customer: I'm calling about the delivery for Saturday morning, just to confirm the details.
K Assistant: No problem. I'll just enter the details into the computer, if you bear with me a moment.

L Customer: Thank you, Katja. You are very efficient. I'm sorry if I sound fussy.
M Assistant: Just a moment, please. I'll call up your order on my database. Yes, we're bringing the flowers at 8 am and we'll put them in the hotel lobby and the conference room, as you requested.
N Customer: Thanks again. Goodbye.
O Assistant: Yes, we've made a note of that.

b) *Listen and check.*

Task 3 Making promises

a) *In both phone conversations, the assistant says 'I'll' or 'we'll' several times. Find the sentences and translate them into German.*

Language tip
Use 'will' when you offer or promise to do something.

b) *Respond to the statements on the left with the phrases on the right.*

1. I haven't got your phone number.
2. I haven't got a fax machine.
3. This box is too heavy for me.
4. This jacket is too big.
5. I don't know where the butter is.
6. I'd like to order some of these.
7. The music is too loud.

OK, I'll ...
Don't worry, I'll ...

- carry it for you
- give you my business card
- show you. Just follow me.
- turn it down
- make a note of the details
- get you a smaller size
- send you an email

Task 4 On the phone

Collect useful phrases for making telephone calls from the dialogues.

Note
→ Find more about telephone skills on pages 130–132.

STEP B – Everyday English

Task 1 Talking Shop

Here are some examples of what sales assistants ask, tell or offer their customers.

I often have to ask customers for their name and address.

I sometimes have to ask them to fill in forms.

I once had to tell someone not to take the product out of the packaging.

a) *What about you? Note down what you …*

- ask customers for, or ask them to do.
- tell them to do, or tell them not to do.
- offer them, or offer to do for them.

I always offer customers a carrier bag.

At Christmas, I offer to gift-wrap presents.

b) *Compare your experience with others in your class.*

Task 2 Customer service: Polite questions

a) *Which of these two assistants has the best way of talking with customers? Say why.*

Give me your name.

May I have your name, please?

Where do you live?

Could you tell me where you live?

b) *Match the halves of the questions*

1. May I	a) sign here, please?
2. Would you please → e)	b) washed the pullover?
3. Could I ask you to	c) smoking in here?
4. Would you mind	d) have your credit card details, please?
5. Would you mind not	e) take your child away from the power drills?
6. Could you tell me how you	f) waiting a moment, please?

c) *Which of the first halves in (b) could you use with the questions below?*

1. … squeezing the oranges?
2. … need the power drill for?
3. … using the stairs? The lift is out of order.
4. … installed the hard drive?
5. … fill out this form, please?
6. … leave your dog outside the store?

Language tip

Would you come back in five minutes, please?

Would you mind coming back in five minutes?

d) *Make the questions more indirect with 'Do you know …?' or 'Could you tell me …?'*

1. What are you looking for?
2. Which model of computer is it?
3. Which brand do you prefer?
4. When do you usually finish work?
5. How does it work?

Task 3 Customer service: Polite responses

Say 'no' politely to these questions. Give a reason with 'I'm sorry, but …' or 'I'm afraid …'

1. Can I pay by credit card?
2. Could you get me a smaller size, please?
3. Do you give discounts to students?
4. Can I smoke in here?
5. Can you ship to the USA?
6. Do you mind if I bring my dog in here?
7. Can I try out this power drill?
8. Haven't you got anything cheaper?

Task 4 Translation

Translate these sentences into German. Then, without looking at your book, translate them back into English. Compare your translations with the original sentences.

1. Apple has launched a new laptop.
2. We haven't got that model in stock.
3. Could you confirm the details in writing?
4. Please bear with me while I enter the details in the computer.
5. I'll just make a note of your phone number.
6. Would you like me to gift-wrap the candle?
7. By the way, how much does it cost?

Task 5 On the phone: Role play

Follow the instructions for the role play. Try to use the polite phrases you have just practised.

Sales assistant at Techno-Market	**Caller**
1. Greet the customer politely →	2. Respond, and ask if the sales assistant speaks English.
3. Say that you do. →	4. Ask if Techno-Market sells the new IKON digital camera.
5. Say there aren't any in stock at the moment, but more have been ordered. →	6. Ask how long it will take before they arrive.
7. Say that it could take about two weeks. Offer to let the caller know by phone as soon as they arrive. →	8. Say you'll think about it. (You want to call Techno-Market's competitor!)
9. Say you have a similar model in stock called the Hot-Shot. It's on special offer, at only half the price of the IKON. →	10. Say that you'd like to come and see it on Saturday. Ask the sales assistant to put one by for you.
11. Ask for the caller's name and address. →	12. Give the caller the details she asks for.
13. Check that you have noted the details correctly. →	14. Say that the details are correct.
15. End the call and say goodbye. →	16. Say goodbye.

STEP C – Written communication

Task 1 Customer enquiry

You work at the information desk at the Stuttgart branch of the ***Morath*** *chain of department stores. This email arrives in your in-box. Read the email and answer the questions below.*

From: Minnie Lee <m.lee@mynet.com>
To: <info_stores@morath.com >
Date: Fri Nov 18, 2009 09:24:33 AM PST
Subject: Le Creuset casserole set

Dear Sir / Madam,

I found your email address on the Morath website, and I am writing to you because I recently bought a set of three Le Creuset casseroles at your Frankfurt branch. They were on special offer at a price of €89.99 for the set, and came together in a Christmas pack.

I am currently staying in Stuttgart but I will be flying home to Hong Kong next week, and I would like to know if you have the same offer in your store. I want to buy another set to take back as a Christmas present, in the same special pack if possible. The casseroles I bought were orange, but I would like to know if you have the dark blue ones in stock.

Please reply as soon as possible, because I will only be here in Germany until Thursday, 24th November, and I would really like to have the casseroles by then.

I look forward to hearing from you.

With best regards,
Minnie Lee (Mrs)

a) *Answer the questions. Be careful with the tenses.*

1. Who sent the email?
2. Where is she from, and where is she staying at the moment?
3. How did she get Morath's email address?
4. What has she bought from Morath before, and from which branch?
5. How much did she pay for it?
6. What does she want to know and why?
7. Why should you reply as soon as possible?
8. What is the best way (email / letter / phone call) to reply, and why?

b) *What should you do before you reply to the customer?*

Task 2 Mediation: A note from the kitchen department

You have checked with a colleague in the kitchen department, and he put this note on your desk.

Summarise in English what the note says. Start like this:

'We have already sold out of the Christmas packs of dark blue casseroles, but we have two sets left in red. Our branch in Frankfurt …'

(Go on.)

Alle dunkelblauen Weihnachtssets sind bei uns schon ausverkauft (zwei Sets sind noch in Rot da). Unsere Filiale in Frankfurt hat noch ein 3er-Set vorrätig. Machen Sie der Kundin folgende Vorschläge: Entweder bestellen wir das 3er-Set von Frankfurt, und die Kundin holt es von uns in Stuttgart ab (Lieferzeit 3–5 Tage). Oder Frankfurt sendet es direkt nach Hongkong (Aufpreis für Porto etwa €15). Sonst kauft die Kundin die drei Casseroles als Einzelstücke (Gesamtpreis €107,97).

Markus

Task 3 Writing for work: Offer

a) *Write a reply to the customer. Follow these steps:*
- Thank the customer for her email.
- Start with the bad news (Unfortunately, …)
- Then give the good news (However, …). Explain what you can offer the customer, and make the different options attractive. You want to make a sale!
- Ask the customer to let you know her decision as soon as possible.
- End with a friendly sentence. (We look forward to …)

b) *Compare your replies. What would you do if you were the customer?*

Task 4 Sounds and spelling

a) *Find the pairs of words that have the same sound.*

hear • sent • rap • right • threw • ~~wood~~ • we'll
there • write • through • scent • weather • their • ~~would~~
wrap • here • wheel • whether

b) *Choose one word from each pair to complete the sentences.*
1. I **would** like to buy some **wood** to make some shelves.
2. When you ...... a letter, it's important to get the spelling ....
3. ...... need to buy a new ...... for your bike.
4. Please come over .... I can't ...... you.
5. I'll listen to some ...... music while I ...... the Christmas presents.
6. He ...... me a bottle of my favourite ...... for my birthday.
7. Do you know ...... the ...... will get better?
8. Someone ...... a stone ...... the window.
9. Those children over ...... should be with ...... parents.

Task 5 Over to you

Work in pairs. Read the situations and decide who will be the customer and who will be the sales assistant. Prepare by writing the dialogues, or just improvise. To help you, some useful phrases are given.

1.

The customer bought a pair of shoes yesterday, but after wearing them for a few hours decided that they were too small. The assistant can change them, but it will take five days to get the bigger size of shoes from the central warehouse.

These shoes are too ...	*Have you got the receipt?*
May I exchange them for a bigger size?	*We can ..., but I'm afraid ...*
How long will it take?	*Which size do you want?*

2.

The customer is interested in buying jewellery. All the best pieces are kept in a locked cabinet for security reasons. The assistant can open the cabinet, but only when another assistant is present. The colleague is at lunch, but will return in ten minutes.

I quite like the ...	*Yes, of course, but I'm afraid ...*
Could you show me the ...?	*Would you mind ...?*
How much is the ...?	*What are you interested in?*

3.

The customer wants to buy a case of expensive wine, but would like to taste it first. This is usually not possible, but there is a wine-tasting at 3pm in the Food Hall, and the assistant suggests that this would be a good opportunity to taste the wine and discuss it with experts.

I'm interested in the ...	*I'm afraid we don't usually allow customers to ...*
Would it be possible for me to ...?	*Would you mind ...?*
That sounds like a good idea. I think I'll ...	*What would you like me to do?*

4.
The customer would like to buy a Black Forest cuckoo-clock and asks if the store can send it directly to the USA by post. The assistant says that this is possible, but explains that there will be an extra cost, and that an insurance form will have to be filled in because the clock is fragile.

I'd like to buy a ...	*Yes, that would be no problem at all.*
Could you ...?	*There is a small extra charge for shipping, and ...*
How much do you charge for ...?	*Could I ask you to ...?*
Do you have the form in English as well?	

LEARNING SKILLS – Learning vocabulary

Task 1 Are you a good language learner?

How you learn a language depends on ...
- whether you like the language
- why you need it
- how often you use it
- what type of learner you are (e.g. Do you prefer to hear and say words before you read them?)
- how you write down new vocabulary

In other words, it depends on YOU!

Are you a good language learner? Discuss the points above with a partner.

Example: *Do you like English? Why do you need to learn it?*

Task 2 Remembering new vocabulary

a) *Each of the tasks below shows a different way to remember new vocabulary. The first seven are tasks to do on your own. The rest are ones you can do with a friend or colleague.*

To do on your own

1. Say these words and phrases below loudly and clearly.

a great bargain • organic vegetables • though • good value for money
convenient • browse • order • I'm afraid we haven't got any in stock
recommend • Would you like me to put some by for you?

2. Do you know what they all mean? If not, make a note and either look them up or ask someone else to explain.
3. Copy the new ones onto small pieces of paper and put them where you can often see them.

> **Learning tip**
> Writing and saying words helps you to remember them.

4. Invent codes or pictures that help you remember them.
5. Copy the ones you might forget easily on to flash cards. Write the German translations on the back. Test yourself regularly.
6. Write a very short text (story or conversation) in which all of the words appear.
7. Memorise the text. Practise it little and often.

To do with someone else

> **Note**
> → Find more tips for learning vocabulary on pages 19 and 33.

8. Test your partner on all the words and phrases.
9. Write a list of 20 words or phrases you have just learned and would like to remember. Test each other until you know them by heart.
10. Write a typical conversation between a customer and a sales assistant. Practise it together and record yourselves on a cassette. Listen to the recording and give each other tips on pronunciation.
11. Talk to each other in English all the time!

b) *Which of these things do you already do? Which will you do in future?*

c) *Have you got any other good learning tips? Share them with people in your class.*

WORD POWER

Task 1 Fill in the gaps

a) *Choose from the words in the box to complete the sentences.*

> *curiosity • deal • avoid • price tag • exclusive • budget*
> *bargain • bother • ditherer • overspend • browse • sales*
> *whim • discount • features • deliver • fragile • supply*
> *organic • perishable • security • biological • safety*

1. I don't want to buy anything. I just want to ....
2. A good time to buy Christmas cards is in the January .... They're much cheaper!
3. We can give you a 2% .... if you pay within ten days.

4. These shoes are a ....! They're only €5.99.
5. How much is this watch? It hasn't got a ....
6. I'm a terrible .... It takes me so long to decide.
7. I'd like to try on those shoes, just out of ....
8. My mum spends €500 in the supermarket every Saturday. That's her weekly food ....
9. The jewellery is kept in a locked cabinet for .... reasons.
10. The clock is extremely ...., so it should be handled with care.
11. Floribunda is going to .... KK Consulting with floral displays for their conference room.
12. I always buy .... food and products made of natural materials .

b) *Write sentences with the words that are left.*

Task 2 How long ...?

Work in pairs. Ask and answer questions about how long things usually take you.

get dressed • have breakfast • get to college / work
do your English homework • make a sale • ...?

Money Matters

4

Content

STEP-IN – Money and numbers

Task 1 The FIZZ-BUZZ game

a) *Can you work out when to say FIZZ and when to say BUZZ?*

'One – two – three – four – FIZZ – six – seven – BUZZ – nine – FIZZ – eleven – twelve – thirteen – fourteen – FIZZ – BUZZ – seventeen – eighteen – nineteen – FIZZ – twenty-one – twenty-two – twenty-three – BUZZ – FIZZ – twenty-six – twenty-seven – twenty-eight – twenty-nine – FIZZ – thirty-one – BUZZ – thirty-three – thirty-four – FIZZ – …

b) *At the start of the game, everyone stands up. Go round the class counting, putting in FIZZ and BUZZ at the right moments. Anyone who makes a mistake is 'out' and has to sit down. The other players start counting again from 'one'. The winner is the last person still standing.*

Task 2 Talking shop

a) *When did you last buy the items on the shopping list? Can you remember what you paid for them?*

b) *Guess the average prices of the items on the shopping list. Add up the prices, and then work out the total.*

c) *Compare your totals. Who has the highest/the lowest amounts? Discuss the differences between the results.*

Shopping list

1 litre milk
6 white bread rolls
2 packets butter (250g each)
1 bottle washing-up liquid
10 eggs
1 kilo potatoes
2 cartons whipping cream
300g ham (sliced)
Small bottle extra virgin olive oil
3 tins ravioli
1 jar raspberry jam

Language tip

We write: 2 packets butter
We say: two packets of butter

Task 3 Facts and figures

British	*American*
tin	can
a pound note	a dollar bill
jam	jelly
value added tax	sales tax

Say the numbers you see in the pictures.

Example: Picture four shows a one-hundred-dollar bill.

Task 4 Listening: Numbers

a) *Write down the numbers you hear.*

b) *Can you remember what the questions were? Listen again to check.*

Task 5 Over to you

a) *Write a list of ten numbers that mean something to you, e.g. your mobile number, your birthday, your height in centimetres.*

b) *Work in pairs. Dictate your numbers to your partner. Try to guess what each other's numbers refer to.*

Example: *Is sixty-three your height in centimetres? – No, it's my weight in kilos!*

STEP A – Shopping

Task 1 At the sales

Sally and Ben are shopping in the January sales. Read the dialogue and answer the questions on page 56.

Sally: I really like that beige handbag. It's twenty per cent off.

Ben: Do you really need a new handbag, Sally? You've already got about ten.

Sally: No, I've only got five, and they're all dark brown. I need a beige one to go with my new shoes.

Ben: Oh, I didn't know you'd bought some new shoes. Did you get them in the sales, too?

Sally: Yes, they were on special offer. They were originally a hundred euros (€100), but I only paid seventy-five euros (€75) for them. That means I saved twenty-five euros (€25)!

Ben: You can't resist a bargain, can you, Sally?

Sally: It's better than paying the full amount, and I'm sure they'll put the prices up again after the sales. Look, that briefcase has been reduced from three hundred euros (€300) to two hundred and fifty euros (€250)!

Ben: Huh! If they can reduce it by that much, it shows how overpriced they were before!

Sally: You're such a skinflint, Ben. Anyway, I'm going to buy some tights. I'm always running out of them, and they've got a good deal at the moment.
You can get two pairs for the price of one.

Ben: While you're doing that, I'm going to ask for some advice about the suitcases. I need a bigger one.

Sally: I'm sure there are some big reductions on the suitcases, too,

Ben: Well, if they aren't on sale, I'll just ask the manager to give me a discount.

1. The beige handbag was originally €50. How much is it now?
2. If Sally buys the beige handbag, how many will she have altogether?
3. How much were Sally's shoes reduced by? (%)
4. How much has the briefcase been reduced by? (€ + %)
5. What product on special offer does Sally decide to buy, and why?
6. What will Ben do if there aren't any reductions on the suitcases?

Task 2 Listening: Shopping for a suitcase

Ben has seen some suitcases that he likes. A sales assistant is helping him.

a) *Find out:*
- *the prices of the three suitcases that the assistant shows him.*
- *other special offers that the assistant mentions, and their advantages.*
- *what Ben decides to do in the end.*

b) *Listen again and note down useful language. Some of the phrases in the conversation are given below.*

Useful phrases: Talking about prices

Customer	Sales assistant
How much is it / How much does it cost?	It's excellent value for money / It's a good price.
That's a bit expensive.	It comes with a guarantee.
It's more than I was expecting to pay.	It's on special offer/on sale.
Does the price include sales tax / VAT?	You get two for the price of one.
Is delivery included in the price?	If you buy two, you get one free.
Is there a discount on that?	It's 10% off the normal price.
How much has it been reduced by?	That's the sale price. We can't reduce it further.
Do you give cash discounts?	It's been reduced by ... That's a reduction of ...
Could you come down a bit on the price?	We've dropped our prices radically.
That's more than I can afford.	The price includes delivery and installation.
Have you got anything cheaper?	If you think it's too much to pay in one lump
That sounds reasonable.	sum, you can always pay in instalments. It's no problem.

Task 3 Prepositions

Put in the missing prepositions.

from • *at* • *for* • *by* • *off* • *to* • *on* • *out* • *of* • *in*

1. Ben's printer has run .... paper. He bought two packets ...... the price ...... one.
2. All the cookery books are 30% ....
3. One suitcase has been reduced ...... €70, ... €199 ...... €129.
4. The suitcase he really liked wasn't ...... sale.
5. He asked ...... a discount, but he didn't get one.
6. There wasn't a discount ...... the suitcase he was interested ....
7. Sally paid only €4 ...... four packets of tights.
8. They're excellent value ...... money.
9. You can pay ...... instalments.

Task 4 'Pay' or 'pay' for'?

Example: You pay for the shoes. You pay an amount.

1. the shoes	5. the rent	9. a dress
2. an amount	6. the flat	10. tax
3. a meal	7. a bill	11. a charge
4. a high price	8. $ 60	12. books

Language tip

pay + money word / request for payment
pay for + what is bought

Task 5 Sales talk 1

A customer is interested in the price of a washing machine.

Customer / **Sales Assistant**

1. Sagen Sie, dass diese Waschmaschine ziemlich teuer ist.
2. Erwidern Sie, dass sie ein gutes Preis-Leistungs-Verhältnis hat.
3. Sagen Sie, dass Sie nicht mehr als €700 ausgeben wollen. Kann man am Preis noch etwas machen?
4. Erklären Sie, dass der Preis schon sehr günstig ist, Sie können keinen Rabatt gewähren.
5. Fragen Sie, ob der Preis die Lieferung enthält.
6. Erklären Sie, dass der Preis nicht nur die Lieferung sondern auch die Installation enthält. Natürlich nehmen Sie auch das Altgerät zurück.
7. Sagen Sie, dass €900 trotzdem viel mehr Geld ist, als Sie ausgeben wollte.
8. Bieten Sie Möglichkeit einer Finanzierung an.

Task 6 Sales talk 2

Work in pairs. ***Student A*** *sells clothes and needs to buy furniture.* ***Student B*** *sells furniture and would like to buy clothes.*

Step 1: *Prepare by inventing some prices and special offers for the items in your shop window.*
Step 2: *Student B asks Student A about prices of items in the clothes shop and tries to get a good deal.*
Step 3: *Change roles, so that Student A is now the customer in the furniture shop.*

Task 7 Paying bills

Match the English words and phrases with the German ones on the right.

invoice net gross quantity unit price total amount customer number receipt order date payable within number of items value added tax/sales tax order description of articles size delivery charge currently valid	Anzahl Teile Kundennummer Brutto Mehrwertsteuer Beleg / Quittung / Kassenbon Bestelldatum Bestellung / Auftrag Größe derzeit gültig zahlbar innerhalb Versandgebühr Gesamtsumme Rechnung Einzelpreis Netto Menge Artikelbeschreibung

Task 8 Customer service: Explaining a receipt

a) *Look at the receipt on the right and answer the questions.*
   1. When and where was the receipt issued?
   2. How many items did the customer buy?

b) *You are the sales assistant. Frau / Herr Seeburger, and the customer asks you to explain the information on the receipt. What do you tell her? Start like this:*

   'You've bought one pullover, and the unit price is ...'

Modehaus Benz
Marktstr. 1
78086 Brigachtal
Tel. 07721 23123
Fax 07721 23124
Filiale: 1 *** Kasse: 3
25.11.2008 12.05 Beleg 243340
Es bediente Sie: Seeburger

IDENTNR.	MENGE	EINZELPREIS	GESAMTPREIS
Pullover (V37)			
0064379	1	39,95	39,95
Bluse K (V37)			
00626547	1	59,00	59,00
Hemd (V38)			
0042343	2	19,00	38,00
Anzahl Teile:	4		
SUMME BRUTTO: (EUR)			136,95
19,0 % MwSt. v. EUR 136,95			26,02
SUMME Netto: (EUR)			162,97

Task 9 Telephone role play: The wrong delivery

Student A
You work in the customer service department of *Stella Versand*, a mail order house that offers delivery for orders over €200. A customer calls you.

Student B
You have just received some goods you ordered but the skirt is the wrong colour and you wanted the set of three towels at €45, not the set of four towels at €55. Also, you thought delivery was free. Call *Stella Versand* and complain.

False Friend
rock ≠ Rock

Stella Versand **Rechnung** **Datum:** 25.11.2009

Alle Preise enthalten die derzeit gültige gesetzliche MwSt.

Kunden-Nr. 2467 Bestelldatum 20/11/06 Bestell-Nr. 6607 Rechnungs-Nr. 23124

Artikelnr.	Größe	Farbe	Artikelbschreibung	Preis (EUR)
132HG	38	dunkelblau	Rock	76,00
334HG	M	hellgrün	Handtuchset	55,00
Versandkostenanteil				3,00
Gesamt:				135,00
MwSt. 19 %				21,60
Gesamt				157,60

Zahlbar innerhalb 30 Tagen netto
Lieber Kunde, vielen Dank für Ihren Auftrag. Falls Sie Fragen haben, rufen Sie uns bitte unter unserer gebührenfreien Telefonnummer an: 0800 9191100.

STEP B – Problem at the checkout

You can leave your purchases here, but I'll have to cancel what I've rung up.
So will I have to go through the checkout again when I come back?
Yes, I'm afraid so.
Hi, Emma Can I lend you the money?
Kevin, what a surprise! That's very kind of you Are you sure?
No problem!
I've only got a € 200 note, I'm afraid.
That's OK. Have you got twenty-five cents?
Yes, here you are.
Here's your change. Sixty-eight euros.
Thanks.
Kevin, if you come with me to my car, I can pay you back now.
Do that later, Emma. I'm in a hurry.
Then I'll give you an IOU note.
May I borrow your pen, please?
Yes, of course.
Bye, Kevin! Thanks!
Bye, Emma!
Kevin, I owe you € 132,25 Emma
Silly woman!
They should open another checkout!
Excuse me, but this fell out of your coat pocket.
Oh, thank you very much.

Task 1 Customer service: Dealing with payment problems

Read the story and answer the questions.

1. Why can't Emma pay for her purchases?
2. Where is Emma's money really?
3. Why does the checkout assistant ask Kevin for 25 cents?
4. What does
   - Kevin lend Emma?
   - Emma borrow after Kevin pays?
   - Emma give Kevin, and why?
   - a customer give Emma?

Language tip

Lend or borrow?
Can you **lend** me $5? ('give')
Can I **borrow** $5? ('take')
If you borrow money you need to give it back (You **owe** it.)

Task 2 Talking shop

a) *How do your customers normally pay?*

in cash • by credit card
by debit card • by bank transfer
by direct debit • by cheque

b) *What problems do customers sometimes have when they are paying for goods?*
Compare your experiences.

Task 3 Talking point

When customers pay by credit card, they have to sign the receipt. Why is this important, and why should you check the signature?

Language tip

Kontrolliere die Unterschrift.
Check the signature.

Unit 4 Money Matters

STEP C – Wrong invoice

Heutelstr. 46
78086 Brigachtal
25th November 2009

Techno-Markt
City Rondell
78054 VS-Schwenningen

Re: Sharp AQUOS LC-13E1E LCD Television – Invoice number 17706/06

Dear Sir / Madam,

I bought a Sharp AQUOS flat-screen LCD television from your branch of Techno-Markt three weeks ago. I have installed it successfully and I am very satisfied with the user-friendly programming controls and the high-quality picture.

Today I received an invoice that seems to contain a mistake. As I do not read German, I asked my neighbour to explain it to me. The invoice asks me to pay the first of six monthly instalments as agreed in the contract I signed when I purchased the television. The total price of the television is €1200, and the monthly instalment requested in the invoice is €200.

However, when I bought the television on 4th November I made a down-payment in cash of €300 (25% of the total price), so the amount outstanding is €900. This means that the six monthly instalments should be €150, not €200. A copy of the receipt you gave me for the down-payment is enclosed.

I am also returning your invoice, and would ask you to correct it and send it back to me for payment.

I look forward to hearing from you.

Yours faithfully,

Jim Sears

Enclosure

Language tip

deposit / down-payment
Anzahlung

Task 1 Summary

Complete the summary below with the details in the box.

€150 • €200 • €300 • €900 • €1200
six • down-payment • satisfied • receipt (x2) • contract
Techno-Markt • flat-screen television • 4th November
Schwenningen • invoice (x2)

On ...., Jim Sears bought a .... from the .... branch of ...., and he is .... with his purchase. However, when he bought it, he signed a .... in which he agreed to pay the total price of .... in .... monthly instalments. At the same time, he made a .... of .... in cash, for which he was given a .... In his opinion, he owes the store ...., which he should pay in monthly instalments of .... Therefore he was surprised to receive an .... from the store asking him to pay .... as a first instalment. In his reply, he encloses both the .... and a copy of the ...., and asks the store to correct the mistake before he pays.

Task 2 Writing for work: Reply to customer

Your boss has asked you to reply to Jim Sears. Follow his instructions:

Ich gehe morgen auf Geschäftsreise. Bitte verfassen Sie einen unterschriftsfertigen Brief (natürlich auf englisch!) an Herr Sears nach folgende Angaben:

1. *Bedanken Sie sich bei Herr Sears für seinen Brief (Bezug auf Rechnung).*
2. *Erklären Sie, dass wir der Sache nachgegangen sind. Scheinbar hat die Buchhaltung einen Fehler gemacht (schreiben Sie "The error was an oversight on our part"), da die Anzahlung offensichtlich nicht berücksichtigt wurde.*
3. *Fügen Sie eine berichtigte Rechnung über €150 bei. Bestätigen Sie, dass die restlichen Zahlungen je €150 betragen. Schlagen Sie die Möglichkeit der Zahlung per Lastschrift (bequemer!) vor und legen Sie die entsprechenden Formulare bei.*
4. *Entschuldigung. Bitte um Verständnis.*
5. *Höfliche Schlussformulierung.*

(Ich unterschreibe nach meiner Rückkehr in drei Tagen).

Note

→ Useful phrases for letter-writing on pages 133/134.

Task 3 Customer service: Telephone role play

Jim Sears
You are still waiting to hear from Techno-Markt. Call them to ask whether they have received your letter. If they have received it, find out what they plan to do about the invoice.

Sales assistant
You have written the letter to Jim Sears, but you have not sent it yet. You get a phone call from Mr Sears. Apologise about the delay in replying, but tell him the good news.

Task 4 Sounds and spelling

a) *In the word 'knife', the letter 'k' is silent. Which are the silent letters in these words?*

1. receipt
2. debt
3. height
4. wrap
5. sign
6. hour
7. comb
8. scent
9. Christmas
10. salmon

b) *Listen and check.*

WORD POWER

Task 1 What you can do with money

Fantastic prizes!
Enter our Christmas competition and win a £500 voucher to spend in our store.

Save the Children Fund
Please donate generously.

Shoplifters who steal items from this store will be prosecuted.

Save $$$ and lose weight. MATFIX' fitness bikes now only $349.99!

Debts? Cash-flow problems? Our in-store bank may have the solution for you. We can lend you $50 a month interest-free. If you need to borrow more, you pay only 2 % interest on the additional amount. Just pay back what you owe at the end of every month.

Due to counterfeit money in circulation we regret that we cannot accept £1000 notes.

Invest in your child's future. Give them a head start with Earlylearn educational software. Don't waste time!

Please count your change carefully.

Cash-machine
Select and press 'ENTER'.
- Deposit cash
- Withdraw cash
- Transfer amount
- Exchange

If you run out of cash, there's no need to run out of the store – you'll find a cash machine on every floor.

a) *What can you do with money? Find verbs in the notices that you can add to this mind map.*

b) *Can you think of any more verbs to add to your mind map?*

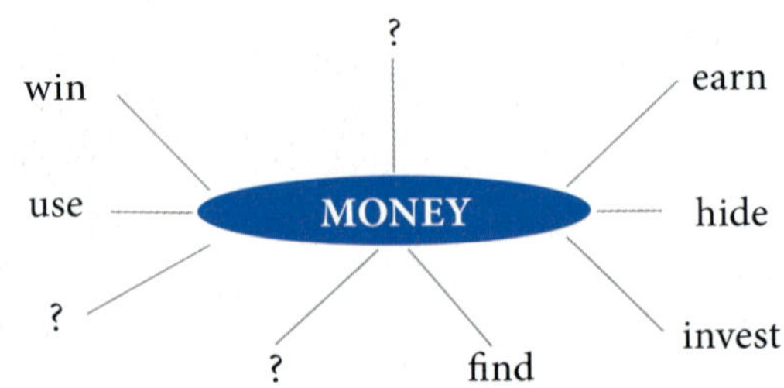

Task 2 Word families

Give the noun forms.

1. to pay
2. to compete
3. to donate
4. to weigh
5. to solve
6. to invest

Task 3 Same word, different meaning

Translate the sentence pairs into German.

1. Don't spend too much time.
   Don't spend too much money.
2. He ran out of the room.
   He ran out of money.

Task 4 'Over'

Make words with 'over'. The first one has been done for you.

1. Someone who has withdrawn more money from a bank than allowed is **overdrawn**.
2. People or things that are too heavy are **over ...**
3. You should try not to **over ...**, or buy more than you can afford.
4. People who earn too much money (more than is fair or reasonable) are **over ...**
5. If you have paid more than the amount on the price tag, you have been **over ...**
6. Things that cost too much or that do not give value for money are **over ...**

weight
spend
paid
priced
~~drawn~~
charged

Task 5 Who does what?

What do sales assistants and customers do? Make two lists. (Some activities can go in both lists.) Add more examples.

spend money • provide information • dither
wrap up presents • ~~browse~~ • give advice
buy things on a whim • look for bargains
explain how things work • try on clothes
compare products • ask for credit card details
~~offer help~~ • try to get a bargain • make a sale
take products out of the packaging
ask lots of questions • offer a carrier bag
put price tags on products • sign receipts

sales assistant	customer
offer help	browse
...	...

Task 6 People and money

Sort the expressions into the right groups.

People who are careful with money …	People who are careless with money …
• save it	• waste it
• …?	• …?

save it • waste it • often run out of cash • usually count their change
invest it • buy things on a whim • spend it on useful things
lend money and forget to ask for it back • know how much they have
never need to borrow it • often check their bank balance • lose it
have cash-flow problems • can pay back their debts
don't notice if they are overcharged • look for bargains and discounts

CHECK-OUT 2

A Sales talk

a) *Match the parts to make questions.*

1. Can I
2. Have you
3. Would your mother
4. Would you like
5. What sort of price range
6. What colour do

a) do you have in mind?
b) got anything particular in mind?
c) me to show you their new range
d) you think she would like?
e) be interested in a silk scarf?
f) help you in any way?

b) *Write a dialogue between a sales assistant and a customer. Use the questions above and these responses.*

B Prepositions

Complete each sentence with one of the words below and a preposition. Be careful with verb forms.

demand • supply • stock • ~~special offer~~ • spend • depend
pay • interested

1. Great bargains! We have lots of fantastic products **on special offer**.
2. I'm afraid we haven't got any … at the moment, but we can order some.
3. There's always a lot of … video games just before Christmas.
4. I … about €100 a week … shopping.
5. I'll … the meal. You're my guest!
6. The price … the quality.
7. Floribunda … hotels and restaurants … floral displays.
8. Are you … organic products?

2 CHECK-OUT

C Different words, same meaning

Say it a different way. Choose from the words below. Be careful with the verb forms.

collect • confirm • deliver • wait • call • launch

1. Could you **phone** me when it arrives?
2. I'll **pick it up** from your store on Saturday.
3. Our new range will be **introduced on the market** in March.
4. Could you **bear with me** for a moment?
5. I'd like to **double-check** the details.
6. We'll **bring** the flowers to your store in the morning.

D Customer service

Suggest ways to make these sentences more polite.

1. Give me your name.
2. Where do you live?
3. Don't squeeze the apples.
4. Weigh the potatoes.
5. How did you hear about our special offer?
6. Fill in this form.
7. Don't use this lift. Use the other one.
8. Why don't you like the shirt?
9. What's your size?
10. Give me the pen.

E The right option

Choose the correct (or better) option.

1. I look forward to (hear / hearing) from you.
2. Would you mind (waiting / to wait) outside for a moment?
3. Good morning. (I'm calling / I call) about the new Apple laptops.
4. Just a moment, (I check / I'll check) the details on my computer.
5. Excuse me, where's the manager's office? – Come this way, (I'll / I'm going to) show you.
6. Could you tell me when (the store opens / does the store open)?
7. It is important to (check / control) the customer's signature.

F Translation

a) *Translate into English.*

1. Vielen Dank für Ihren Auftrag.
2. Enthält der Preis Mehrwertsteuer?
3. Sie dürfen Ihre Einkäufe hier lassen.
4. Sie können den Betrag überweisen.
5. Das Preis-Leistungs-Verhältnis stimmt.

b) *Translate into German.*

1. You get two for the price of one.
2. We'll have to ask for a down-payment.
3. Do you ship to the USA?
4. I'm afraid we don't accept €1000 notes.
5. Please keep your receipt.

Advertising and Promotion

5

Content

STEP-IN – Celtic Dragon

A new gift shop called Celtic Dragon is about to open in Nuremberg in June, at the height of the tourist season.

Grand opening next week!
Celtic Dragon –
Myths, Legends and Quality Gifts

Our finest selection of gift ideas from Scotland, Ireland and Wales.

- Traditional wool: scarves, capes and hats
- Scottish Tartan: kilts, bags, socks in a range of colours
- Leather: belts, boots, waistcoats, sporrans
- T-shirts: Braveheart, Dragon, Merlin, Arthur (all sizes)
- Island Crafts: art in pottery, glass, jewellery and copper
- Books: castles, warriors, myths and magic
- Fine Foods: biscuits, cakes, whisky, salmon, fudge
- Music: bagpipes, harps, CDs of Scottish & Irish music
- Soft toys: dragons, ravens, Loch Ness monsters

Open on Saturday 3rd June at 10am. Free glass of wine or Guinness!

An alle Mitarbeiter

Sie haben eine tolle Arbeit geleistet, aber es gibt noch eine Menge zu tun! Das Rock im Park-Fest findet am Wochenende statt und es kommen viele Rock-Fans aus allen Herren Ländern nach Nürnberg – eine super Gelegenheit auch für uns! Wie können wir diese potenziellen Kunden zur Celtic Dragon locken? Ideen und Anregungen sind willkommen!

Patrick O'Connor
(Geschäftsleiter)

Celtic Dragon

High Quality Imports
Clothing, Jewellery and Leather
Gifts and Fine Foods
Myths and Legends

Celtic Dragon, Königstr. 2, 90459 Nürnberg

The Celtic Knot

Fine hand-crafted silver with the famous knot design of the ancient Celts

- ➩ *magic rings and armbands*
- ➩ *necklaces and bracelets*
- ➩ *coins and medals*
- ➩ *plates and goblets*
- ➩ *silver cutlery sets*

All ***Celtic Knot*** jewellery is guaranteed solid sterling silver and is marked 'Made in Scotland'

Enter our fabulous whisky quiz! Free!

Just answer these three questions about whisky and you might be a winner!

1. What is the difference between whisky and whiskey?
2. What cereal is the basic ingredient of whisky?
3. The word 'whisky' comes from Scotland's Gaelic language – what does it mean?

Tick the three 'answer boxes' on the back of this leaflet, include your name and contact details and give your entry to our sales staff in the store. The winners will be announced on Saturday 10th June at 3pm.

Prizes

1st prize: A trip to one of the famous Speyside distilleries in Scotland.

2nd prize: Two tickets to the 'Irish Firedance' performance in Berlin.

3rd prize: A silver 'Celtic Knot' whisky flask and a bottle of 12 year-old whisky.

CELTIC DRAGON LAUNCH PARTY

You are invited to a VIP breakfast to celebrate the launch of our new speciality store.

Time: *9am on Saturday, 3rd June*

Venue: *Celtic Dragon roof-top garden*
Königstr. 2, 90459 Nürnberg

smoked salmon
–
scrambled eggs
–
organic oatcakes
–
Irish breakfast bacon
–
selection of fine teas

Join us for an informal breakfast at our new cafe above the store – a chance to enjoy some Scottish and Irish specialities and to meet the press on our big opening day. The store will be officially opened to the public at 10am.

Task 1 Opening a new store

Read the texts and find the answers to these questions.

1. Who is Patrick O'Connor?
2. What famous event is happening this weekend, and who will be there?
3. What has Patrick O'Connor asked his staff to do?
4. What do you think will he be doing on Saturday at
   (a) 9.30 am? (b) 10.15? (c) 3 pm?

Task 2 Typical products

What products and foods are typical of Scottish, Irish or Welsh culture? Collect ideas from the texts.

Task 3 Listening: Radio commercial

Patrick O'Connor is advertising the opening of his store on Foxx FM, a local Nuremberg rock station.

Listen to the commercial and find out what sort of people he hopes will come to the store.

Task 4 Talking shop

a) *Work in groups and discuss ideas for promoting the store this weekend. Think about these points:*
   - where to distribute the 'grand opening' flyer around town
   - what rock festival fans might want to buy
   - what other groups of customers might want to buy Celtic Dragon products

b) *What promotional activities does your store organise?*

STEP A – Promotion at the rock festival

You work at the Nuremberg branch of *Route 66*, a chain of stores selling American jeans and accessories. Your boss has decided to promote these products at a stand inside the *Frankenstadion* for the *Rock im Park* event.

Task 1 Matching words

Match the adjectives on the left with the products on the right. (Some of the adjectives could describe more than one product.)

high-heeled • studded leather heavy denim • spotted designer • genuine snakeskin stonewashed • Mexican silver checked • hand-crafted	bandanas • cowboy boots belts • earrings • jackets hatbands • jeans • buckles shirts • necklaces • vest cowboy hats • bracelets

Task 2 Writing for work

a) *Work in small groups. Design a poster and a leaflet for the Route 66 stand. Use ideas from Celtic Dragon's advertising campaign, but try to create a Wild West look. Start by discussing these points:*
- What images make people think of the Wild West?
- What images of the Wild West are connected to rock music?
- Which ones could you use in your poster / flyer?

b) *Discuss the best places to distribute the leaflets, and where to display the posters.*

What do you know about Route 66? Find out more on the internet. What makes it a suitable name for a company selling jeans?

Task 3 Talking shop

Work in four groups. In your group, decide on ways of attracting people to your stand.

Group 1
Bar-B-Q Grill

What 'Wild West' food will you serve?
(Don't forget food for children and vegetarians.)
What else will you offer? (e.g. free drinks if people buy one of your products)

Group 2
Wild West quiz

Write a quiz with three questions about the Wild West.
List three prizes (first, second and third) of Route 66 products.
Decide when / how the winners receive their prizes. (Main stage of *Rock im Park*?)

Group 3
Lucky Dip

Can anyone try the lucky dip, or do they have to buy something first? Minimum purchase €1.
What will you put in the lucky dip? (small gifts, vouchers, etc.)
What is the biggest prize in the lucky dip?

Group 4
Bucking Bronco

A Bucking Bronco is a wild ride on a mechanical horse.
Who may go on the Bucking Bronco? (Minimum purchase or is it free?)
How long does someone have to stay on the horse to get a prize?
What are the prizes?

Task 4 Sales talk: Saying the right thing

You are offering free samples of a spicy Mexican dip for people to taste. *Decide which phrases would be suitable to use with the customer on the left, and on the right. Are there any that you could use with both customers?*

- Hi, how are you? Try this new …!
- Excuse me, could I interest you in this?
- Go on. Take one, it's really tasty!
- Excuse me, we're promoting a new product.
- They look good, don't they? Try one!
- Good morning, would you care to sample this?
- May I introduce our new product line?
- So … what do you think of them?
- I think you will find these rather interesting.

Task 5 Sales talk: Promotions in the store

Read the conversations and say whether the customer is very interested, unsure or not at all interested.

1.

Assistant: Hello, would you like to try this new Mexican Chilli dip?
Customer: Thank you, it looks interesting.
Assistant: What do you think?
Customer: Whew! It's quite spicy. What's in it exactly?

2.

Assistant: Excuse me, would you like to enter our raffle?
Customer: Oh yes please, I like raffles. What can I win?
Assistant: We're promoting French Week. First prize is a case of wine from the Bordeaux region.
Customer: That sounds great! I hope you give me a lucky ticket. What do I have to do? And will there be a wine-tasting, too?

3.

Assistant: Hi! Can I offer you one of these Belgian chocolates?
Customer: They look fantastic. But I have a nut allergy, so no thanks!
Assistant: We have some without nuts. Finest quality 100 % chocolate.
Customer: No, I'd better not. I don't want to be ill!
Assistant: OK, I understand. Have a nice day!

Language tip

I'd better not =
I had better not

I'd rather not =
I would rather not.

Task 6 Over to you: Role play

Practise product promotions with a partner. Take it in turns to be the assistant and the customer. You can choose from the ideas on the right, or a promotion that you have in your own place of work.

organic yoghurt • incense candles
low-alcohol wine • Celtic key-rings
cherry tomatoes • nutty bread-sticks

STEP B – Explaining products

Task 1 Listening: In-store announcements

You will hear two in-store announcements.

a) *Listen to the first announcement and correct the wrong information in the leaflet on the right.*

b) *Listen to the second announcement and note down answers to these questions:*
   1. Where should customers go to get the in-store card?
   2. What are the benefits of the card?

c) *Use your notes to write a leaflet about the in-store card.*

FREE WINE-TASTING!

A free wine tasting will be held today in the Food Hall on the ground floor. At 4 pm, a guest speaker will give a short talk about some famous wines from the Rhineland region. Customers will have the chance to buy crates of wine at discount prices, and three types of snacks will be offered: cheese, sausages and fruit.

Task 2 Mediation: Filling in an application form

You need to help a customer fill in an application form for a store card.

a) *Match the expressions on the form with the questions on the right.*

1. Anrede / Titel
2. Staatsangehörigkeit
3. Straße und PLZ
4. Wohnhaft in ... seit
5. Familienstand
6. Art der Wohnung
7. Berufliche Angaben
8. Bruttohaushaltseinkommen
9. Bankverbindung
10. Gewünschte Verfügungsrahmen für die Bezahlkarte
11. Datum / Unterschrift

a) What is your employment status?
b) Could you give me some details about your accommodation?
c) What is your gross annual income?
d) Could you sign here please, together with the date?
e) What is your address and postcode?
f) How long have you lived at this address?
g) What is your nationality?
h) What is your marital status? For example, are you single or married?
i) Could you give me your banking details, please?

j) What title would you prefer? (Mr, Mrs, Ms, Dr, etc.)
k) What is your credit limit request? For example, the minimum is €250, and the maximum is €1000.

b) *The points below are on the same form. How would you ask the questions?*

Name und Vorname • Geburtsdatum • Anzahl der Kinder
Telefon (Festnetz) • Telefon (Mobil) • Arbeitgeber/Firmenname

c) *Here are some of the customer's answers. What would you write on the form, and where?*

I live in a rented flat • My account number is 2183112, but I can't remember the sort code. • I'm divorced. I earn about €60,000 a year. I don't have any children. • I'm an American citizen.

d) *Visit the homepage of an international retail chain (e.g. IKEA) and download the English and German versions of the store card application form. Work in pairs and explain to your partner how to fill in the German form. (The English version will help you with vocabulary.)*

Task 3 Mediation: Explaining instructions

A customer is interested in a cheese cake mix, but can't understand the German instructions.

Explain the instructions in English.

Useful phrases

to preheat the oven to …
to lightly grease a tin / pan
to line with greaseproof paper
to dust with flour
to beat the ingredients on low / medium speed
to pour the mixture into the tin
to bake for … minutes
to allow to cool before …
Best before / Use by (+ date)

Zubereitungsanleitung

1 Backofen auf 180 Grad vorheizen. Kuchenform einfetten und mit Mehl bestäuben oder mit Backpapier auslegen.
2 Kuchenmix, 240 ml Wasser, 120 ml Pflanzenöl und 3 große Eier 30 Sekunden auf kleiner Stufe mit dem Mixer verrühren. Dann 2 Minuten auf mittlerer Stufe verrühren.
3 Den fertigen Teig in die Kuchenform geben und im Backofen 27–33 Minuten goldbraun backen. Lassen Sie den fertigen Teig vor dem Schneiden und Servieren auskühlen.

Task 4 Mediation: Explaining a label

A German-speaking customer is interested in a new skin care cream, but some important information on the label is in English.

How would you answer this customer's questions? What else could you tell her?

'Olive oil' ist klar – das ist Olivenöl, oder? Aber was heißt 'pomegranate'?

Ich kaufe ausschließlich Naturprodukte. Sind alle Bestandteile pflanzlichen Ursprungs?

Meine Haut ist besonders empfindlich. Manchmal bekomme ich furchtbare Ausschläge.

Und wie sieht es aus mit Tierversuchen?

Leider ist meine Haut eher zu fett als zu trocken. Ist es das richtige Produkt für mich?

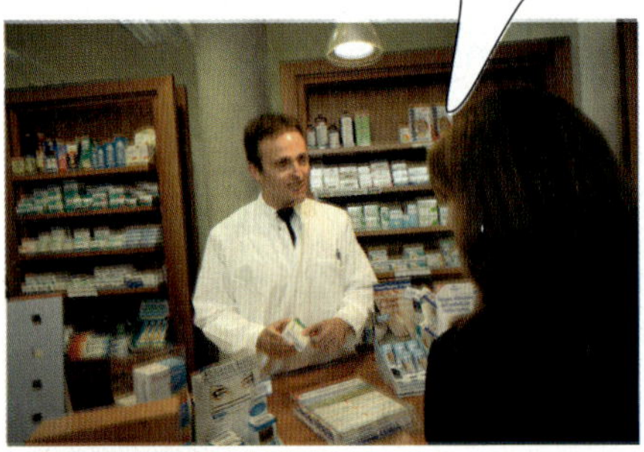

STEP C – Promoting yourself: Applying for a job

One day you may want to apply for a job in an English-speaking country, or where English plays an important role. A curriculum vitae and an application letter in English will help you to 'sell yourself'.

Celtic Dragon

VERKÄUFER/INNEN GESUCHT

Teilzeit, evtl. auch Vollzeit
(25 / 40 Std. in der Woche)

Laden für Originalprodukte aus Schottland, Wales und Irland sucht engagierte und kontaktfreudige Verkäufer/innen mit guten Englischkenntnissen, um unser dynamisches Verkaufsteam zu unterstützen.

Sie haben eine erfolgreich abgeschlossene Berufsausbildung und sind kommunikativ, zuverlässig, teamfähig, einsatzbereit, flexibel und belastbar. Bei uns finden Sie ein tolles Arbeitsklima mit der Möglichkeit für Weiterbildung.
Lohn / Gehalt: nach Vereinbarung

Interessiert? Dann bewerben Sie sich schriftlich mit Lebenslauf und Zeugnissen bei Patrick O'Connor, Celtic Dragon, Königstraße 2, 90459 Nürnberg

Job category:	Retail
Job type:	Sales Assistants
Location:	Dubai
Reference#:	RTL-0045

Description: We are a leading fashion and sportswear retailer with three new branches in the exciting and cosmopolitan city of Dubai, and we are looking for enthusiastic and experienced sales assistants. As well as greeting the customers and offering them advice and information to keep them satisfied, you will also be involved in keeping the shop tidy, and checking and replacing the stock.

Requirements: You have excellent customer care skills and fluent English; you enjoy meeting people and have two years' retailing experience.

Salary: negotiable

Task 1 German ➔ English

Translate the Celtic Dragon job advertisement above into English.

Task 2 Pros and cons

a) *Work in groups. Compare the three vacancies and discuss the pros and cons of each one.*

b) *Which job would attract you most? Explain why.*

Task 3 Your dream job

Write an advertisement for your dream job.

Christkindl Shop

Vacancy for Sales Assistants

Christkindl is a rapidly expanding retail chain specialising in Christmas gifts and decorations made in Germany. We have recently opened a new branch in the popular English seaside resort of Brighton and have a vacancy for a young and ambitious sales assistant with experience of selling and a good knowledge of English and German.

Apply with CV and covering letter to Julie Watson, Manager, 34 Brunswick Terrace, Brighton BN1 9QU, by 30th June.

We are an equal opportunities employer

Task 4 A letter of application

a) *Put the verbs in the right form.*

Application for Vacancy as Sales Assistant

Dear Ms Watson,

I (*write / am writing*) to apply for the vacancy as sales assistant, which (*was advertised / has been advertised*) in yesterday's edition of The Guardian.

As you can see from my enclosed CV, I (*will become / am becoming*) a qualified sales assistant at the end of this year. I (*currently do / am currently doing*) an apprenticeship at a large department store, and I (*attend / was attending*) classes once a week at a vocational college.

The reason why I (*apply for / am applying for*) a job in Brighton is that my girlfriend (*has just started / just started*) a new job in a bank there and we (*get married/will get married*) in England next year. Although I (*never worked / have never worked*) in a store like yours, I am sure that I have the necessary skills for selling gifts and souvenirs. As far as my language skills are concerned, I (*learn / have been learning*) English since I (*was / am*) ten years old. Also, I (*spent / have spent*) three weeks in Brighton as an exchange pupil.

If you *(think/will think)* I am the right person for the job, I *(would be / have been)* pleased to come to Brighton for an interview.

I look forward to *(hear / hearing)* from you soon.

Yours sincerely,
Markus Schilling
Enclosed: CV and certificates

Note

→ Find more about tenses in the Grammar Hot Tips section.

b) *Do you think Markus has a good chance of getting the job? Why / why not?*

Task 5 Role play: Interview

a) *Work in groups. Discuss what information should go in a CV, and write a list of headings, e.g. 'Personal Details' or 'Education and Training'.*

b) *Find someone from another group to work with. Interview him / her using your headings for ideas.*

Example: 'What is your name?' • 'Where did you go to school?' • 'What languages do you speak?'

Task 6 Writing for work: Your CV

a) *Look at the model CV and application letter on pages 135-137. In what ways would yours be different?*

b) *Write a CV and application letter for one of the jobs advertised on the previous page, or for your dream job.*

BrE: curriculum vitae
AmE: résumé

STEP D – A new store

Task 1 Opening a new store

a) *As a result of the successful promotion at the Rock im Park festival in Nuremberg, the Route 66 retail chain has decided to open a new store in Stuttgart.*

Complete the following invitation, which will be sent out to VIPs and the local press.

Jeans, Jackets and Accessories

Genuine Western Wear***

You are i.... to the grand opening of our new Stuttgart store .... 15th August .... 10 am.

We will have a wide r .... of speciality western fashion clothing on display, in .... jeans, jackets, vests and cowboy hats. We also offer high q.... leather goods imported directly from Arizona, USA.

Come and join us in the store and meet the press. Our sales s.... will be serving drinks and snacks, and will be happy to answer all your q.... and show you our exciting selection of products.

The launch party will be held .... Monday and the store will open to the public .... Tuesday. All our guests will be offered special offers, including BOGOF promotions, and you can be the first to get one of our special storecards.

Route 66 will be open daily .... 9.30 am .... 6 pm.

Alexanderstr. 66, 70182 Stuttgart

Language tip

on Saturday
at eleven o'clock
in the morning
on (the) 15th July
from 9am to 5pm
until (up to) Friday

Note

→ Find more about tenses in the Grammar Hot Tips section.

What does **BOGOF** mean?

Buy One ...

b) *The boss of Route 66 wants to know what the guests think of the new branch, and has asked you to write a questionnaire to give guests as they leave the party. It should give feedback on the following points:*

- the Route 66 range of western clothing and accessories

- the location of the new store in Stuttgart city centre
- the interior design and layout of the store
- the welcome by the staff and the management
- any other ideas or suggestions they would like to add

Design a questionnaire with clear, simple questions. Add further questions that could provide useful information for promoting the new store, and offer guests a free gift as an incentive to fill in the form.

Note

→ Find more about question forms in the Grammar Hot Tips section.

Task 2 Everyday English

At the in-store promotional event, the sales staff are welcoming visitors and making small talk.

Can I leave my coat somewhere?

Yes, I live in Chicago.

Hello. Can I get you something to drink?

Yes, please. They look delicious!

Cheers!

Are you staying here in Stuttgart?

Pleased to meet you.

I'm sorry, you'll have to smoke outside, I'm afraid.

I've been employed here for nearly a year.

Yes it is. I really like it here.

Match what people say with the questions / responses in the box below.

Of course. I'll hang it in the cloakroom.	Would you like to try a prawn snack?
Yes, we're staying at Hotel Graf Zeppelin.	How long have you worked here?
Cheers!	Could you give me an ashtray, please?
How do you do?	Are you from the USA?
I'd like a white wine, please.	Is this your first visit to Germany?

Task 3 Listening: What would you say?

At the launch party, different people come up to talk to the sales assistants.

Listen and for each person suggest what you could say to keep the conversation going.

Task 4 Customer talk: A launch party

a) *Brainstorm ideas for a launch party that would bring as many people into the store as possible. Here are some things to consider:*

Store layout • Special offers • Displays • Music • Party events
Snacks & drinks • Celebrities and VIPs

b) *Turn your classroom into a launch party for the Route 66 store. Divide into two groups, one group of sales assistants and one group of visitors to the store:*

Sales assistants	Visitors
Welcome your visitors, offer them a drink and a snack and make small talk. Find out what products interest them, point out the special offers you have, and draw their attention to the launch party events you have organised.	Decide what type of customer you are, and what Route 66 products you might be interested in. Ask about any special offers that might be part of the launch promotion, and make sure to move around and meet as many people as possible.

WORD POWER

Task 1 Odd one out

Which is the odd one out? Say why, and put the 'wrong' word in the 'right' group.

1. case, harp, piano, trumpet
2. plate, jug, bowl, leather
3. box, crate, bagpipe, carton
4. boiled, wool, cotton, nylon
5. scrambled, fried, mug, smoked

Task 2 Words in context

a) *Complete the gaps with the missing words. (There are more words than gaps).*

satisfied • spend • branch • selection • choose • purchase
tasteful • prizes • hook • ingredients • cutlery • accessories
satisfying • prices • cloakroom • tasty

1. We have an exciting ...... of products on display.
2. Have you bought all the ...... to make the cheesecake?
3. It's important to keep customers ....
4. Christkindl has just opened a new ...... in Brighton
5. I never win ...... in raffles.
6. May I have another of those biscuits? They're very ....

7. You have to spend at least €10. That's the minimum ....
8. Give me your coat. I'll hang it up in the ......

b) *Write sentences with the other words.*

Task 3 False friends

Suggest a better word for the 'false friends'.

Example: We want to invite ~~the prominence~~ to our VIP party. = celebrities

1. What's wrong? You don't look very ~~lucky~~.
2. This Mexican dip tastes very ~~sharp~~.
3. A kilt is a type of ~~rock~~ with a tartan pattern.
4. Please ~~control~~ the leaflet for mistakes.
5. My grandmother will get her ~~rent~~ when she's 60.
6. This cream is for dry and ~~sensible~~ skin.
7. You can pay the invoice amount in ~~rates~~.
8. How much interest will I have to pay on the ~~credit~~?
9. Information about the product is given on the ~~etiquette~~.

Note

→ Find more about false friends on page 189–191.

Sales talk step-by-step

6

Contents

STEP-IN – Selling

Task 1 Comparing leaflets

a) *Compare the two leaflets on the next page – the type of store, the products and the way they are advertised.*

b) *What other products would you expect to find in each store?*

Task 2 Listening

Listen to the conversations. Are the customers in DIY WORLD or LIFESTYLE? Say how you know.

Task 3 Talking point

Compare the type of customers who shop in the two stores. How might selling to each type be different?

Task 4 Sales talk: Phrases for phases

An assistant in the carpet department of LIFESTYLE is talking to a customer.

a) *Match what the assistant says with the phases of the selling process.*

Phase 1	Phase 2	Phase 3	Phase 4
→ Making contact with the customer	→ Finding out the customer's needs	→ Presenting the goods	→ Bringing the sale to a close

b) *You will find more phrases as you go through the unit. Note down and practise the ones that are especially useful to you at work.*

Task 5 Talking shop: Ten top tips for selling

a) *Talk about the sales tips. Are there any you don't agree with? Explain why.*

TEN TOP TIPS

1. Greet customers by name if possible.
2. Don't talk too much. Maintain a dialogue with the customer, and be a good listener.
3. Avoid questions that might be answered with 'no'. Use open questions where possible.
4. Show customers no more than three or four items to choose from.
5. Explain to the customer how the product meets his or her needs.
6. Speak in everyday language.
7. If a customer asks 'How much does it cost', don't just state the price. Explain how the product offers value for money.
8. Be confident about offering articles in a higher price range.
9. Avoid using the words 'cheap' and 'expensive'.
10. If a customer decides against making a purchase, show that you respect the decision.

b) *Add more tips of your own.*

STEP A – Dealing with customers

Task 1 Making contact with the customer

What would you say to the customers in each case? Choose from phrases in the box below:

Learning tip

Useful Language

- Good morning.
- Can I help you?
- Would you like to look around?
- Are you looking for anything in particular?
- Hello, I see you're looking at … / looking for …
- Would you like a closer look?
- Would you like me to show you how it works?
- Feel free to take them off the shelf.
- Would you like to try it on?

Task 2 Talking point: Tricky situations

a) *Do customers in your store ever pick up, feel, unpack or even try out products by themselves? How do you react when they do?*

b) *Discuss which of the following goods customers should be allowed to touch or handle:*

clothing • tools • dried flowers • books • soft fruit • aerosol sprays
electrical goods • porcelain • unwrapped foods • toys
jewellery • antiques • mobile phones • knives • pens • glass
computers • house plants • bikes

Example: 'Customers should be allowed to handle or touch antiques.'
'Yes, but it depends on how fragile they are.'

Task 3 Finding out customers' needs

Read the dialogues and answer the questions below.

Florian Müller, a sales assistant at DIY World, sees a man looking at power tools.

Florian: Guten Tag.
Customer: Oh, good morning. Er … do you speak English?
Florian: Yes, that's no problem. Are you looking for anything in particular?
Customer: Yes, I want a power drill, but I don't know if any of these are big enough.
Florian: Well, what do you need it for?
Customer: I'm restoring an old house. So I'll have to drill into stone, concrete, steel and wood.
Florian: The one you are looking at is the top of the range. It's powerful enough to do all those jobs, and more. Let me show it to you.
Customer: It looks very nice, but it is rather expensive.
Florian: It's a cordless drill, so you can use it anywhere. The price includes two batteries and charger, and a carrying case with all the accessories you need.
Customer: How long does it take to charge the batteries?
Florian: Thirty minutes. And that will give you five hours of drilling work, while the second battery is charging. So there's no need to worry about cables.
Customer: A cordless drill. That sounds interesting. Is it complicated to use?
Florian: No, it's very user-friendly. But it does come with a manual.

Julia Loy, a sales assistant at Lifestyle, sees a woman looking at tablecloths.

Julia: Good morning. Those are lovely tablecloths, aren't they? Provençale printed cotton.
Customer: They're gorgeous. Do you have any round ones?
Julia: Yes, we do. Square, oval and rectangular. What size do you have in mind?
Customer: It would be for our dining room table, which is huge. We like to give big dinner parties.
Julia: And what's the colour scheme of your dining room, if I may ask?

Customer: Well, I'm trying to create a Mediterranean look – bright colours, but tasteful – not garish.
Julia: These tablecloths are all classic French designs, from the Aix region. Look, what do you think of this one? It's got the traditional olive leaf pattern in warm reds and browns.
Customer: Hmm … the fabric feels wonderfully soft. And are the colours natural?
Julia: Yes, they are. You can see the North African influence.
Customer: And who makes these tablecloths?
Julia: Papillon. You can tell from the little butterfly logo in the design. They also do table napkins to match the tablecloths. Would you like me to show you?

a) *Which of the two customers fits these descriptions? Say how you know.*
- price-conscious
- brand-conscious
- looking for something versatile
- hoping to impress other people
- concerned about the environment
- interested in technical details
- interested in style and design
- likely to buy what the assistant offers

b) *Work with a partner. One person reads the customer's or the assistant's questions while the other person – without looking at the book – tries to remember the responses.*

c) *Here are some responses. What are the questions?*
1. Yes, I'm looking for a desk light for my office.
2. Yes, I would. Is there a changing room?
3. No, thank you. I don't like nuts.
4. I'll pay by credit card.
5. I'm buying it for my daughter.
6. No, thanks. I'm just looking.

STEP B – Presenting goods

Task 1 Making a sales pitch

Match an expression from each column to show which product is being sold.

STEP 1: Refer to the features of the product.	STEP 2: Explain the benefits of the product.	STEP 3: Make it an experience to look forward to.
They're rich in iron and vitamin C.	So you can set it in advance.	You'll feel warm even in sub-zero temperatures!
It's made of T400-Garn.	Red peppers help prevent colds.	You'll be able wake up to the smell of freshly-baked bread.
It also has a timer function.	It's as soft as most other fleeces, but it's water-resistant and four times as windproof.	Your family will stay healthy during the winter months.

Task 2 Appealing to the senses

Complete the sentences with a verb and an adjective. (The first one has been done for you.)

look – taste – feel sound – smell	+	sweet – slim – soft – younger – tinny – spicy hard – fresh – bad – powerful

1. This cashmere jumper **feels soft**, just like a baby's hair!
2. This ...... very .... It's got too much sugar in it.
3. That black dress makes you ....
4. Loudspeakers that ...... are usually the cheaper brands.
5. If fish ...... , you shouldn't eat it.
6. If the mango ...... , then it isn't ripe yet.
7. A bit of extra curry powder will make the sauce ....
8. Olive oil face cream will make you ....
9. Some drivers prefer loud engines because they ....
10. Spray it in the kitchen and the air will ...... again.

Language tip

Use adjectives to say how something **is, seems, looks, feels, tastes**, or **smells**.

Task 3 Say it another way

Respond using different combinations of the words in bold, as in the example

1. The **bread** is so **fresh**! Do you **bake** it in the shop? – Yes, we always sell **freshly-baked bread**,
2. And the **juice** tastes so **fresh**. Do you **squeeze** it just before serving? Yes, the juice is always …
3. The **design** of the **engine** is **brilliant**. Well, it is a …
4. The **cut** of this **suit** feels **wonderful**. Yes, it's a …
5. Are these **chocolates made** by **hand**? Yes they're …
6. The **training** of your **assistants** seems **very good**. – That's true. They're …

Task 4 Explaining benefits

Complete the sentences with an adjective or an adverb.

1. You can apply the paint *(easy/easily)*.
2. The paint dries very *(quick/quickly)*.
3. It's an *(economical/economically)* washing machine.
4. These protective goggles ensure that you work more *(safe/safely)*.
5. With this tool, you can drill into brick more *(accurate/accurately)*.
6. This stretch fabric allows you to move your arms *(easier/more easily)*.
7. These cushions will go *(good/well)* with your sofa.
8. The napkins will look *(good/well)* with your tablecloth.

Language tip

It's an **efficient** machine. (adjective)

It works **efficiently**. (adverb)

Learning tip

fabric ≠ Fabrik

Task 5 Talking about cost

a) *Some vowels (a-e-i-o-u) are missing from some of the words. Can you guess what the words are?*

1. This is a **hgh-qlty** washing machine that works very **effcntly**, yet it's very **rsnblyprcd** at only €849, it's very **ecnmcl** to run and has hardly any **bckgrnd** noise.
2. This anorak costs only €399 yet it is **wndprf**, **drbl** and offers **excllnt prtctn** against all sorts of weather if you want to go hiking this weekend. It's great value for money.
3. This power drill is of **prfssnl qlty**, and the **adjstbl** controls allow you to drill **esly** and **accrtly** into cement ceilings, yet it costs only €199! As you can see, it's quite a **brgn**!
4. This parmesan cheese is nine months old and it tastes **absltly dlcs** with any pasta dish because of its **intns flvr**, yet it costs only €3.49 for 100 grams.
5. Medipharma Cosmetics skin cream is **nnvtve** and **rch** in **ntrl** ingredients. It will make your skin feel **sft** and **smth**, and if you apply it **rglrly**, you'll look ten years **yngr** after just ten days, yet it costs only €59.49 a jar.

b) *Collect phrases from the sentences that are useful for talking about (and around) the price.*

Task 5 Over to you

a) *Write a sales pitch for one of the following articles, or for one offered in your shop.*

b) *Work with a partner. Practise your sales pitches on each other, taking turns as the assistant and the customer. When the customer asks for the price, remember to repeat the benefits of the product.*

Useful phrases: Presenting the goods

Referring to product features
- It is made of …
- They are rich in …
- It has a …
- It contains …

Describing benefits
- The material makes it …
- You can …
- It helps/allows/enables you to …
- This product ensures that you …

Referring to future experience
- When you …, you'll be able to …
- With this product, you will always …
- You'll find that you can …
- You won't need to worry about …

Appealing to the senses
- Feel how soft it is.
- Doesn't it sound great?
- It tastes delicious.
- Smell this – isn't it wonderful?
- It looks so elegant.

STEP C – Objections

Task 1 Dealing with objections

a) *Match the products on the left with the customers' objections on the right.*

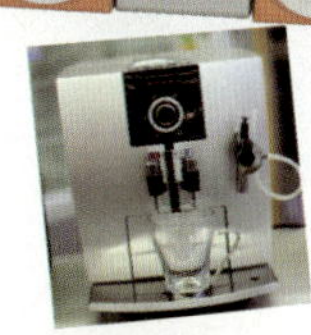

b) *Work in pairs. Take turns responding to the objections, using the phrases in the box.*

- I see what you mean (pause), but …
- I can assure you that it's not a problem …
- That's easily adjusted. Let me show you …
- It's designed to do that, because …
- That can happen with a new machine.
- I understand what you're saying.
- That is very easy to prevent.
- Yes, many customers ask about that.

c) What if the customers are still not satisfied? *Suggest alternative models or brands, and explain why they are better, e.g.*

bigger speakers • better quality • more features • a scratch-free surface • more user-friendly controls • a simpler design • an in-built water softener • longer cables • a more compact version • ...?

You can start like this:

'Let me show you a different model. Although the price is slightly higher, ...'

Learning tip

in a **higher** price range	**easier** to clean
much stronger **than**	(not) **as** heavy **as**
the best available	**the widest** range

Note

→ Find more about comparative forms in the Grammar Hot Tips.

Task 2 Listening: Offering accessories

a) *Before you listen, suggest which accessories could be sold along with the products below.*

b) *Now listen to the conversations and decide which product the customer is buying. Say how you know.*

c) *Listen again and note down the accessories that are mentioned.*

Task 3 Sounds and spelling

Which word is the 'odd one out'? Saying the words aloud will help you.

1. holiday	heavy	hour	high
2. rough	through	tough	enough
3. usual	university	umbrella	user
4. fragile	target	allergy	huge

Task 4 Role play: Offering accessories

a) *What accessories could you sell with the following products?*

MP3 player • vacuum cleaner • sports shoes • barbeque set
ski-suit • chainsaw • house plant • plasma-screen TV • dishwasher
sunglasses • rucksack • laser printer

b) *Work in pairs, taking it in turns to be the customer and the sales assistant. Try to interest the customer in making some additional purchases. The phrases below will help you.*

Learning tip

- Can I interest you in …?
- Would you also be interested in …?
- You already have …, don't you? *(Assistant expects customer to say 'no'.)*
- By the way, we also have some … that match this …
- If you want a … for your new …, we have a wide range available.
- Would you like me to show you some … that you can play on it/use with it?

Would you also be interested in any upgrades for your software?

By the way, we also have some very nice cushions that match this sofa.

If you want a leather case for your new phone, we have a wide range available.

Would you like me to show you some games software that you can play on it?

STEP D – Customers' decisions

Task 1 Helping the customer decide

Look at how these assistants deal with 'ditherers'.

I don't know whether to buy the cheaper lawnmower or the more expensive one.

If you buy a higher-quality product, it will last longer and you'll pay less for maintenance.

I still can't decide between the black anorak and the blue one.

They both really suit you, but the black one will go with anything.

a) *What could you say to help these customers decide?*

I'm interested in this laptop, but it looks complex. I think I might have problems later.

I really like this clock, but it looks too fragile to send back to the USA.

I'm not sure my wife will like these garden gnomes.

These white cushions would look great in my house, but it would be hard to keep them clean.

Task 2 The moment of decision

Which of the statements below show that the customers are ready to buy? Suggest suitable responses, also for those who don't 'bite'.

1. Can you arrange delivery to my home address?
2. Thank you for your help, I'll think about it.
3. Do I need to fill in a form for the guarantee?
4. My wife will kill me when I bring it into the house!
5. I think I would prefer to keep looking, thank you.
6. Is it possible to pay in instalments?
7. I'm afraid it's not quite what I was looking for.
8. Could I have it wrapped as a birthday present?

Useful phrases

If the customer doesn't bite ...
Let me just give you this catalogue.
If you need any further information, please ...
If you don't find what you're looking for, we've got plenty in stock.
If you change your mind, we're still here!
I can understand that you want to think about this.

Task 3 Payment

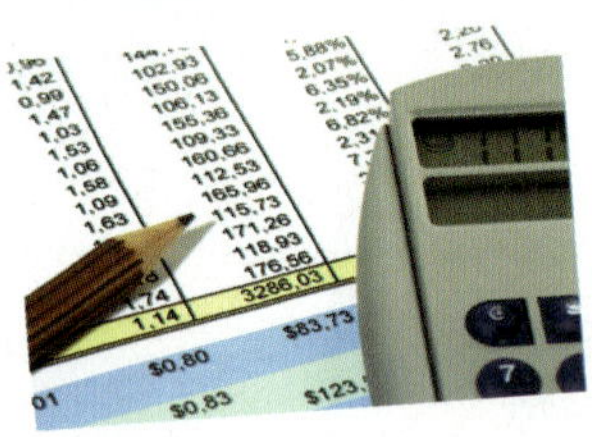

Complete the sentences with words from the box. (There are more words than gaps!)

1. Shall I take the goods to the ...... for you?
2. Are you paying with ...... or by ......?
3. Here's your ......, three euros and twenty-two cents.
4. Keep the ...... in case you want to ...... the goods.
5. Would you like a ...... for that?

invoice • exchange • change • discount carrier bag • credit card charge • cash desk • loan • receipt • cash

WORD POWER

Task 1 Similar but still different

Explain the difference.

1. tiny / tinny
2. sensitive / sensible
3. tasty / tasteful
4. recipe / receipt
5. goggles / glasses
6. waterproof / water-resistant

Task 2 30 point quiz

Do this quiz in teams of three or four. (Some of the answers can be found in this unit.)

1. a) How big is the garden shed on offer at DIY World? (1 point)
   b) Write down how you would say this. (1 point)
2. a) Name the products shown in LIFESTYLE's advertisement on page 65. (1 point)
   b) Give two adjectives from the text that describe the table. (1 point)
3. How long is DIY World open during the day? (1 point)
4. Suggest four possible words to complete this sentence: (4 points)
   'I'm sure you will be ...... with this product.'
   (Tip: the words can begin with 'd', 'h', 'p' and 's'.)
5. What material are Aura products made of? (1 point)
6. Translate the expressions. (6 points)
   a) *Es passt gut dazu.*
   b) *Möchten Sie es anprobieren?*
   c) *Sie können auch in Raten zahlen.*
   d) *Wer ist jetzt dran?*
   e) *Bitte nicht anfassen.*
   f) *Es steht Ihnen sehr gut.*
7. What adjective beginning with 'v' describes a tool that can do many things? (1 point)
8. Say how the following products might taste / sound / feel / smell / look (6 points)
   a) curry
   b) an unripe mango
   c) a powerful engine
   d) a cashmere jumper
   e) perfect skin
   f) meat that has gone 'off'
9. Give an example of a product for each 'objection'. (6 points)
   a) easily scratched
   b) has wobbly legs
   c) doesn't open properly
   d) makes too much steam
   e) is fuzzy
   f) are too tight
10. Which expression means the same as 'in stock' (1 point)
    a) available b) adjustable c) accessible

CHECK-OUT 3

A Describing patterns

Describe the pictures.

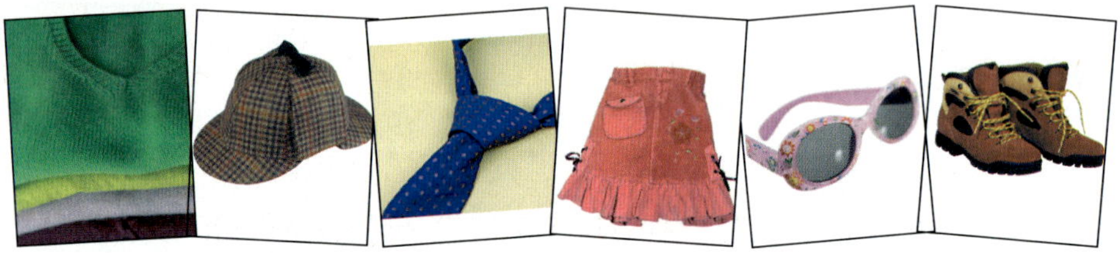

Example: In the first picture, you can see shirts of different colours: …

B Job advertisement

Complete the advertisement with the missing words on the right.

KOCHLINK
1. for Sales Assistant
KOCHLINK is a successful **2.** of kitchenware stores **3.** in Düsseldorf. We have recently **4.** into the UK market and are looking for friendly, **5.** and **6.** sales assistants to work in our new **7.** in Birmingham and London.
8. must have sales experience, an **9.** in kitchenware products, a good **10.** of English and excellent **11.** care skills.
We offer flexible working **12.** and **13.** for further training.
The **14.** is negotiable, depending on experience and **15.** Send your **16.** and certificates to Pete Turner, Kochlinks, Clarry Street, Birmingham B742RA by 15th March.

opportunities • customer • applicants • enthusiastic • hours
knowledge • qualifications • reliable • expanded • chain • branches
interest • curriculum vitae • salary • vacancy • based

C German ➔ English

Translate the following expressions into English.

1. Name / Vorname
2. Staatsangehörigkeit
3. Anschrift
4. Telefon (Mobil / Festnetz)
5. Familienstand
6. Anzahl der Kinder
7. Beruf
8. Arbeitgeber
9. Kreditinstitut
10. Kontonummer
11. Bankleitzahl
12. Unterschrift

D The right option

Complete the sentences.

1. These muffins are really (*tasty / tasteful*). Could you give me the (*recipe / receipt*)?
2. If you have (*sensitive / sensible*) eyes, you should wear (*glasses / goggles*) when you go swimming.
3. The handbag goes (*real good / really good / real well / really well*) with your shoes.
4. The butter tastes (*strange / strangely*). I think it has gone (*of / off*).
5. I love the (*wonderful / wonderfully*) smell of (*fresh-baked / freshly-baked*) bread.

E Prepositions

Put in the missing prepositions

1. ...... 9th January ...... 9am.
2. ...... 10am ...... 6pm.
3. to pay ...... the goods
4. to be ...... stock
5. It depends ...... the price.
6. I'm not interested ...... that.

F One word, different meanings

Translate the words in orange.

1. a) I like the colours of this **suit**.
   b) Yes, warm colours really **suit** you.
2. a) Do you **charge** for delivery?
   b) Who is in **charge** of advertising?
3. a) Is there a **deposit** on these bottles?
   b) I haven't got enough cash with me. If I pay a **deposit**, will you put the dress by for me?
4. a) I'd like to **apply for** a store card.
   b) I'm going to **apply for** a new job.

G Short forms

Write the full forms.

1. DIY
2. BOGOF
3. CV
4. VAT
5. asap
6. USP

H Compound nouns

Match one word from each box to make a new word.

house • aerosol • mobile • curry work • dried • ash • table chain • skin	*cloth • saw • phone • bench tray • plant • cream • flowers spray • powder*

Example: chainsaw

I Questions

Put the words of the sales assistant's questions in the right order.

1. it – whose – is – turn ?
2. to – like – you – try – would – on – it ?
3. or – by – you – credit – cash – paying – card – are – with ?
4. you – cash desk – to – the – I – shall – take – goods – the – for ?
5. for – need – do – what – you – it ?
6. in – for – you – are – particular – looking – anything ?

J British or American English?

a) *Is the speaker using British or American English?*

1. I'm looking for a leather vest.
2. I've only got a one hundred euro note.
3. I've sent my résumé.
4. This jam is delicious!

b) *Give the British / American alternatives.*

On the spot: dealing with special situations

7

Content
STEP-IN – Customer Talk
STEP A – Dialogues
STEP B – Love is priceless, weddings are expensive
STEP C – Rules and regulations
STEP D – An upset customer
WORD POWER

STEP-IN – Customer talk

Task 1 Talking point

Do you find it easy or difficult selling to these customers? Explain why.

clothing • tools • dried flowers • books • soft fruit • aerosol sprays
electrical goods • porcelain • unwrapped foods • toys
jewellery • antiques • mobile phones • knives • pens • glass
computers • house plants • bikes

Example: 'Customers choosing presents are difficult because they often don't know where to start.'
'Well, I think that makes it easier because then you can suggest more things.'
'Yes, but it depends on how much time the customer has.'

Task 2 Listening: On-the-spot

You are going to hear three dialogues between sales assistants and customers.

a) *Match the dialogues with the pictures.*

b) *Listen again to the first dialogue. Describe the situation and the assistant's reaction. What tips would you give the assistant?*

Language tip

If that **happened** to me, I **would apologise** to the customer.

c) *Listen again to the other two dialogues. Explain what happens, and say how you would react if you were the assistant. What exactly would you say?*

Task 3 Matching words

Match the expressions with their German equivalents.

1. It's up to you.
2. It costs a fortune!
3. What a rip-off!
4. I haven't got a clue.
5. He who pays the piper calls the tune.
6. It's very handy.

a) Wer bezahlt, darf auch bestimmen.
b) Ich habe keine Ahnung.
c) Es kostet ein Vermögen.
d) Es ist Ihre Entscheidung.
e) Es ist sehr praktisch.
f) Das ist Nepp!

Task 4 Customer talk: Quiz

Work in pairs. Discuss which is the best response.

1. 'Excuse me, where are the frying pans?'
   a) 'I'm afraid I'm serving someone else, but I'll be with you in about ten minutes.'
   b) 'Can't you see I'm busy? I've only got one pair of hands.'
   c) 'They're on the first floor. If you need any help, let me know.'

2. 'I don't care if my daughter likes the jacket. I'm not going to spend a fortune on something she'll only wear once or twice.'
   a) 'Yes, but if she really likes the jacket, she'll wear it a lot longer.'

b) 'Yes, these designer brands are always very pricey.'
c) 'Well, it's up to you. He who pays the piper calls the tune.'

3. 'I know from experience that you can't put this sort of blouse in the washing machine.
   a) 'Yes, that was true in the past. But nowadays these blouses are machine-washable. It says so here on the label.'
   b) 'No, I have to correct you here. These blouses can be machine-washed.'
   c) 'It's a shame. So many customers make that mistake.'

4. 'You haven't got a clue, have you?'
   a) 'How dare you insult me in that manner!'
   b) 'I'm sorry you feel that way, but I can ask a colleague to help you if you like.'
   c) 'I'm sorry, but I'm new here.'

5. 'That price is an absolute rip-off!'
   a) 'That's your opinion.'
   b) 'Well, I can show you some cheap ones if you like.'
   c) 'Do you think so? If you consider the quality it's excellent value for money.'

6. 'I'd like to have a word with the manager, please.'
   a) 'I'm afraid he's busy.'
   b) 'Why?'
   c) 'Of course. I'll just check if he's free.'

7. 'No, I don't want one of those small alarm clocks. They're rubbish quality.'
   a) 'That's true. The bigger ones are better made.'
   b) 'We don't sell anything that is rubbish quality.'
   c) 'The advantage of the small ones is that they're handy when you're travelling.'

Task 5 Talking shop

Has a customer ever put you 'on the spot', or have you ever been in a situation when you didn't know what to say or do? Ask your partner what he/she would have done.

Language tip

If that **had happened** to me, I **would have apologised** to the customer.

Note

→ Find out more about if-sentences, see Grammar Hot Tips.

STEP A – Dialogues

Task 1 Sales talk: Customers with an 'expert'

Dialogue 1

Assistant: Good morning, can I help you?
Customer: Yes, I'm looking for a new chainsaw.
Assistant: Well, as you can see, we have a good range of chainsaws.
Customer: Yes, you certainly do. I'm sure I can find something here.
Friend: Actually we'd like to look at some Swedish saws. They're the best.
Assistant: Yes, they make very good saws, but we have other brands that offer excellent value.
Customer: Is there a big difference in price?
Friend: You have to pay more for the best. All the top brands are manufactured in Sweden.
Assistant: That's true of the ones used by professionals in forests. But why do you need a chainsaw?
Customer: I need it for various jobs in the garden, and also for cutting up firewood.
Assistant: In that case I'd recommend something easy to handle. Here's a popular model for home use.
Friend: It looks too light to me. Would it be suitable for cutting down trees?
Assistant: It has a 40 mm cutting bar, so it will tackle most jobs. And it's also very quiet.
Customer: Ah, that's an important point. Could you start it up and give me a demonstration?

Dialogue 2

Assistant: Good morning.
Customer: Hello. I'm interested in buying a camera.
Friend: We'd like to look at some quality cameras, not these digital cameras. They're all the same.
Assistant: They're not, actually. They come with a range of different features. The advantage of modern digital cameras is that they're very easy to use. You just point them and press the shutter.
Customer: Well, that's probably what I'm looking for – something simple.
Friend: But digital cameras don't give you the flexibility that a good camera does. You can't change lenses if you want to take a telephoto shot. And you can't adjust the flash.
Assistant: That's not true. I could show you a digital camera that does all of those things, and more.

Friend: So what sort of lens does it have? According to the tests I've read, the problem with digital cameras is the quality of the lens.
Assistant: OK, have a look at this digital camera. It's a top-range Nikon used by professional photographers. It can be fitted with the best lenses on the market.
Customer: It looks quite impressive, but how much does it cost?
Assistant: This camera is one thousand two hundred euros, including lens and battery.
Customer: Wow! That's expensive. I don't think I want to pay that much, just for a camera.
Friend: You see what I mean? If you want a good digital camera, you have to pay a lot of money.

Compare the dialogues. Which one is more successful? Can you say why?

Task 2 Fill in the gaps

Find words in the dialogues to complete these sentences.

1. Many people use chainsaws to .... firewood and store it for the winter.
2. Forestry companies .... trees for furniture and house-building materials.
3. Another way of saying 'to turn on an engine' is to .... it ....
4. Just press the .... on the top of the camera when you are ready to take a picture.
5. This camera can take .... pictures, which make far away objects larger and clearer.
6. To take pictures when the light is low, use the .... to make everything bright.
7. Light enters the camera through the .... , which functions like a human eye.

Task 3 Sales talk: Persuading

Match the parts of the sentences to find ten useful phrases.

1. I see your	a) have just the thing for you.
2. I understand what	b) as the tests are concerned, but ...
3. Yes, you're absolutely right as far	c) the other hand, ...
4. Yes, that's true. On	d) you're saying.
5. What exactly do you	e) need it for?
6. How are you	f) case, I'd recommend this brand.
7. If you're looking for something	g) point
8. In that	h) but it's also on special offer.
9. This model here is not only a top brand,	i) versatile, then let me show yout his model.
10. I think that we may	j) planning to use it?

Task 4 Sales talk: Finding a middle way

a) *Before you listen, look at the picture and say what you think the mother and daughter are saying. How should the sales assistant react in this situation?*

b) *Listen and note down:*
- the kind of shoe the daughter wants
- the kind of shoe the mother thinks she needs
- the solution the sales assistant offers
- how the sales assistant persuades the mother.

c) *Use your notes to act out the situation.*

Task 5 Over to you

Choose roles and act out the following situations. You can prepare by inventing some facts about the products (prices, functions, special features, etc.) that will help you in your discussion.

Role A
You are a sales assistant in Megamarkt, a store selling consumer electronics. You approach two customers who seem interested in DVD players. You can see that one of them appears to be a potential buyer and the other is an 'expert' in electronics.

Role B
You are a keen football fan and you have saved up for a top-of-the-range flat screen TV and DVD player. You have asked a friend who knows a lot about this type of equipment to come along to give you advice.

Role C
Your friend has asked you to help in choosing a new flat screen TV and DVD player. You know a lot about electronics, and you know that your friend has plenty of money to spend, so you have been reading all the tests in the consumer magazines.

STEP B – Love is priceless, weddings are expensive

Task 1 Talking point: The cost of weddings

The cost of a wedding in the UK is estimated at between £16,000 and £25,000. Although fewer people are choosing to get married, weddings are becoming increasingly extravagant.

Are weddings in your country as expensive as in the UK? List the things that are usually needed for weddings, and say who usually pays for them.

Total – £17,200 (approx. €25,000)
Engagement ring – £1,289
Wedding rings – £665
Groom outfit – £242
Bridal outfit – £1,500, including £100 on lingerie
Reception – £6,076
Honeymoon – £2,857

Task 2 Translation: Wedding gift list

Translate the gift list into English. Suggest a price range for each item.

Kaufhaus Morath
Geschenkwunschliste

Bräutigam: Fabian Munz
Braut: Melanie Cooper
Hochzeitstag: Samstag, den 21. Juni

Bad
- Bademäntel
- Badetücher verkauft
- Elektrische Zahnbürste
- Handtücher
- Personenwaage verkauft
- Seifenspender aus Glas

Dekoration
- Bilderrahmen
- Blumenvase verkauft
- Kerzen
- Kerzenständer
- Sofadecke
- Terrakottatöpfe verkauft

Freizeit
- Picknickdecke verkauft
- Picknickkorb mit Geschirr
- Reisekoffer

Küche
- Brotmaschine
- Butterglocke
- Capuccinotassen verkauft
- Champagnerkelche
- Dampfdrucktopf
- Entsafter
- Espressomachine
- Toaster verkauft
- Fischbesteck
- Fondue-Set
- Käseglocke
- Messerset in Messerblock verkauft
- Salz- und Pfeffermühle
- Weingläser

Sonstiges
- Seidenbettwäsche
- Exklusivmarkenuhren verkauft
- Mikrowellenherd

Task 3 Mediation: Choosing from the list

Melanie's friend Paul Brogan from Australia has come to Morath to choose a present.

Follow the instructions for a role play between Paul and the sales assistant.

Sales assistant at Morath	Paul Brogan
1. Der Kunde gibt zu erkennen, dass er angesprochen werden möchte. Sprechen Sie ihn an.	2. Ask if the sales assistant speaks English.
3. Sagen Sie, dass Englisch für Sie kein Problem ist.	4. Explain why you have come. Ask to see the wish list.
5. Zeigen Sie die Wunschliste. Bieten Sie den Kunden an, die Begriffe zu übersetzen bzw. erklären.	6. Accept the offer, but add that you don't want to pay more than €50.
7. Empfehlen Sie einige Artikel.	8. Ask questions about the items.
9. Beantworten Sie die Fragen. Helfen Sie bei der Kaufentscheidung.	10. Say which item you have chosen. Ask to see it.
11. Zeigen Sie den Artikel.	12. Ask if the assistant will wrap it.
13. Erklären Sie, dass es zur Serviceleistung gehört.	14. Thank the assistant.
15. Fragen Sie den Kunde, wie er bezahlen will.	16. Say that you will pay in cash.
17. Den Verkauf abschließen. Verabschieden Sie sich von dem Kunden.	18. Thank the assistant and say goodbye.

Task 4 Telephoning role play

Caller

You would like to buy a wedding present for Melanie and Fabian, who have sent you their wedding list. Unfortunately, you are too busy to go shopping, so you decide to call Morath to order a present. You are prepared to pay up to €100, and you would like the present to be delivered to your home.
When you call, you are put through to a sales assistant. Start by checking if s/he speaks English.

Sales assistant

All of the wedding presents on Melanie and Fabian's gift list have been sold. Your boss has told you that if anyone else wants to buy a present, you should ask the customer about the tastes and interests of Melanie and Fabian, and recommend a suitable gift within the customer's budget.
The phone rings. Greet the customer and deal with his/her requests.

Task 5 Talking point: Choosing presents

Do you think wedding lists are good thing? Or is it better to give 'surprise' presents?

STEP C – Rules and regulations

Task 1 Customer talk: What would you say?

1
You work in a supermarket. You notice a customer pushing a trolley through the store accompanied by two children. The children are arguing and making a lot of noise, so the customer takes two chocolate bars out of the trolley, and gives them to the children to keep them quiet.

2
Rule: No goods are to be unwrapped or consumed until they have been paid for at the checkout.

3
A group of young people are in the music department. They have spent a long time listening to CDs but they are not buying anything. Some of them have rucksacks with them.

4
Rule: Customers are asked not to bring rucksacks or other bags into the CD and DVD section.

5
Two teenagers come to the checkout where you are working. They have beer and cigarettes in their basket. You ask to see an identity card or evidence of age. One of the customers can prove that he is 17, but the other one is clearly under-age and has no proof of identity or age.

6
Rule: No alcohol or tobacco products may be purchased by or on behalf of customers under the age of 17.

7
A customer says that he has no cash and would therefore like to pay for goods using a credit card. The total value of the goods is €7.25.

8
Rule: No payment by credit card can be accepted for purchases under €10.

a) *How would you react in these situations? What exactly would you say?*

b) *Choose the correct word to complete the sentences.*

Useful phrases

I'm sorry, but …
Unfortunately …
I'm afraid you can't …
Excuse me, but …

1. Excuse me, can you (*proof/provide/prove*) that this is your bag?
2. Unfortunately we only (*accept/allow/permit*) payment in euros.
3. Could you please (*sign/signature/underwrite*) this credit card receipt?
4. I'm afraid if you can't (*think/remember/remind*) your PIN number you'll have to pay with cash.
5. I'm sorry, but you can't (*take/bring/have*) your dog in here – animals must stay outside.

Task 2 Over to you

Work in pairs. Take turns being the customer and the sales assistant.

Customer: You want to know if it is OK to smoke in the store while you are shopping.
Customer: You would like to pay by credit card, although you only want to buy a few items.
Customer: You are returning a jacket that you bought and you'd like to have your cash back, but you don't have the receipt.

Sales assistant
In each case decide whether the customer's request fits the rules and regulations of your shop, and respond in a polite way.

Task 3 Talking shop: Shoplifters

Have you had any experience of shoplifting where you work? Describe the tricks that shoplifters use, and say what shops can do to reduce or prevent shoplifting.

Task 4 Listening: An embarrassing incident

a) *Describe what you think is happening in the pictures. Choose from verbs in the box.*

watch • suspect • to follow • stop • arrest • apologise • release
let someone go • pay a fine

b) *Listen to one of the customers, Antje, describing the incident. Find out why …*

1. … the two friends went to Zurich.
2. … they decided to go into the leather shop.
3. … Claudia hung the handbags on Antje's arms.
4. … they left the shop in a hurry.
5. … they had to go back inside.
6. … Antje hadn't noticed the bag on her shoulder.
7. … the store detective let them go.
8. … they decided to try on fur coats.

c) *What questions do you think the store detective asked?*

d) *Write suitable dialogues to go with the pictures and act out the dialogues.*

Task 5 Customer talk: Saying the right thing

What would you say if you (a) suspect someone of shoplifting, or (b) find out that the person is innocent after all? Choose from the expressions on the next page.

STEP D – An upset customer

Read this letter of complaint from a regular customer of a large supermarket. There may be some words you don't know, but try to understand the main points.

The Manager
Marktkauf
Röntgenstr. 34
78048 Villingen

15th December

Dear Sir or Madam,

I am writing to complain about an incident that occurred at your store last week in which I was treated in a humiliating and unprofessional manner by members of your staff.

After I had passed through the checkout I was apprehended by a man who questioned me about the goods I had purchased. When I enquired who he was, he said he was an employee of the store and that he had a duty to search anyone suspected of shoplifting. He insisted on inspecting my bags in full view of other customers, and the assistant on the checkout even asked me to empty my pockets. While they were searching me, a crowd gathered around us, and a large queue formed at the checkout.

Needless to say, no stolen goods were found and my receipt proved I had paid for my purchases. I told your store detective that I wished to make a complaint, but he refused to show me any means of identification. He even said that he should not be criticised for doing his duty. I received no apology from him or the woman at the checkout who had also wrongly accused me.

As a senior citizen of 76 years and a loyal customer of your store, I do not expect to be treated like a criminal. I am still very upset by this experience, and I have not returned to your store because I have lost confidence in your staff and do not wish to be accused again.

Friends and family have advised me to take legal action, but I hope that this will not be necessary. I would appreciate an apology, and an assurance that steps will be taken to avoid such embarrassing incidents in future. I would consider coming back to your store, but only if I can be sure that such a thing would not happen again.

I look forward to a satisfactory reply.

Yours faithfully,

Mrs Edwina Stench

Task 1 Talking point: Dealing with complaints

a) *Explain why Mrs Stench is so upset. Do you think she is right to complain?*

b) *What should the manager of Marktkauf do now?*

Task 2 Everyday English

The day after the incident, Mrs Stench tells a friend about what happened. Find formal expressions in the letter that match the everyday expressions she uses with her friend.

*'**Something** very embarrassing **happened** to me at Marktkauf yesterday. After I'd **gone through** the checkout, a man **stopped** me and **asked me about** what I had **bought**. When I **asked** who he was, he just said he **worked in the shop**. He started to **look carefully through** my bags – even though **all the other customers could see**. Of course, I could show I'd paid for **the goods** with my receipt. He didn't give me his name, and when I asked to see his **ID**, he **said no**. I said **I wanted** to make a complaint, and then he said I shouldn't **say bad things about him** because he was only doing his job! He didn't **say sorry**, and did the checkout lady who **said I had stolen things when I hadn't**. They shouldn't treat an **old person** who has been **a regular shopper** for years like a **thief**! I can't **go back** there again. Do you think I should **get a lawyer**? I hope **I won't need to**. I'll **be pleased** if they just **say sorry** and **promise** to **do what they can so that it won't happen again**. Maybe I'll write a letter to the manager. I hope he'll **give me the answer I want**!'*

Example:
'Something happened' means the same as 'an incident occurred'.

Task 3 Sounds and spelling: Understanding different accents

You will hear two people reading these sentences. The first person speaks with a standard British accent, the second with a standard American accent.

1. It's my duty to report what happened.
2. I called your secretary last week.
3. She told me to write a letter.
4. The store detective did not say he was sorry.
5. Ask your staff not to laugh.
6. I've got a new car.

Listen and say what differences you notice.

Task 4 Writing for work: A letter of apology

Your boss, Herr Willi Maier, has asked you to write a letter in English to Mrs Stench based on these notes:

Bedanken Sie sich bei Frau Stench für den Brief. Wir bedauern sehr, was passiert ist und entschuldigen uns für die Unannehmlichkeiten. Erklären Sie, was wir gemacht haben bzw. tun werden, damit es nicht wieder passiert. Betonen Sie, dass wir Frau Stench als langjährige Kundin sehr schätzen. Bieten Sie ihr einen Gutschein im Wert des Kassenbons (€63) als Wiedergutmachung / Entgegenkommen an. Ich möchte sie zu einem Kaffee einladen, damit ich mich persönlich bei ihr entschuldigen kann. (Frau Stench soll uns bitte sagen, wann sie vorbeikommt.) Beenden Sie den Brief in der Hoffnung, dass sie das Angebot akzeptieren kann.

WORD POWER

Task 1 Make or do?

Two managers are discussing a new trainee, Janie.

a) *Put in make or do. Be careful with the verb form.*

Herr Reinel: Janine hasn't ...... much progress this month, has she?
Frau Hirsch: I think she could ...... better. But she has ...... a bit more effort with her appearance.
Herr Reinel: Too much, in my opinion! Last week she ...... her hair like a Mohican.
Frau Hirsch: She's working harder at college. Her teacher says she ...... her homework regularly now.
Herr Reinel: Yes, but whenever I ask her to ...... me a favour or even a simple task, she always ...... excuses.
Frau Hirsch: Janine has some good qualities, though. She seems to ...... friends easily.
Herr Reinel: Yes, but she ...... long phone calls to them on her mobile instead of ...... her work.
Frau Hirsch: Really? Well, in that case she needs to ...... a choice between her job and her friends.
Herr Reinel: Maybe I ...... a mistake when I hired her. Do you think we should sack her?
Frau Hirsch: You need to ... the decision, Herr Reinel, not me. But if I were you, I'd ...... an appointment with Janine before you decide what to ....

b) *Make a list of expressions with 'make' and 'do'.*

c) *Can you make a rule for when to use 'make' and when to use 'do'?*

make	do
• a list	• a task
• ...	• ...
• ...	• ...

Task 2 Word pairs

a) *Find the pairs that make new words and translate them into German.*

bath • picture • microwave espresso • wedding • pressure wine • picnic • suit • butter candle • pepper • honey digital • chain	*stick • case • glass • frame moon • hamper cooker machine • camera oven dish • towel saw • mill • ring*

Example: bath + towel = bath towel (Badetuch)

b) *Add new words to make more compounds (e.g. bath **mat**, **swim**suit, **bread** stick).*

Task 3 Formal and informal expressions

a) *Rearrange the letters of the formal expressions and match them with the informal ones.*

1. It's extremely **envnonctei**.
2. It is very cpirye.
3. I don't have the information you **ruerIqe**.
4. They are very **ybesraanlo**-priced.
5. I do **plagosoie**.
6. They are of **rrfoniei** standard.

a) It costs a fortune!
b) They're dirt cheap.
c) It's so handy.
d) I haven't got a clue.
e) They're rubbish.
f) I'm sorry.

After-sales

8

Content

STEP-IN – Feedback

Task 1 Talking point

What makes a happy customer? Brainstorm ways in which retailers can keep customers satisfied.

The cost of customers

- It costs five times more to gain a new customer than to keep an existing one.
- 90% of unhappy customers will never use you again unless you deal with their problems.
- Each unhappy customer tells 10–16 others.

Task 2 Listening: A satisfied customer

A satisfied customer is talking to her friend about the furniture and equipment she has bought for her new flat.

a) *List the reasons why the speaker is satisfied with the department store's customer service.*

b) *What was she not so happy about? Suggest what the store could do better.*

Task 3 Talking point: Taking action

a) *What can the store do if goods are faulty? Make sentences about what a store can do if customers complain. (Remember that they can sometimes do more than one thing.)*

Example: If something is the wrong colour, the store can suggest an alternative.

If something is …	damaged flawed the wrong colour / size / type incomplete missing substandard not the quantity ordered delayed lost in transit not functioning properly (or has broken down) …?	the store can …	reduce the price. grant a reduction / discount. give the customer a full refund. take it back to have it repaired. contact the service engineer. exchange it. replace the missing / broken parts. offer a substitute. give the customer a credit note. offer compensation suggest an alternative. …?

b) *What should sales staff <u>always</u> do when customers complain?*

c) *Match each action with an expression.*

Deal with the customer personally Admit the mistake Apologise and empathise Take prompt action Offer compensation Thank the customer	→	Please accept this small gift to make up for it. I'll replace it right away. Thank you for letting us know about this. I'll deal with this problem myself. There has definitely been a mistake. I am sorry. I can see you are angry about this.

Task 4 Talking shop

a) *How do customers usually make their complaints where you work?*

b) *Give examples of what they complain about and how their complaints are dealt with.*

STEP A – At the Customer Service Desk

Task 1 Customers who return products

Read the two dialogues and answer the questions below.

Dialogue 1

Assistant: Good morning, how may I help you?
Customer: I bought this silk blouse here yesterday, and it's got a hole in it.
Assistant: Thanks. Let me have a look at it. Ah, yes, I can see that there's a flaw in the fabric. Would you like to exchange it for another one?
Customer: Yes, but your colleague over there told me you don't have any more in stock.
Assistant: I see. Well, in that case we can either order a new one – it would only take a few days – or we can give you a credit note so that you can choose something similar.

Customer: I'm not really keen on any of the other colours, and I can't wait either. I'm on vacation here from the States and I fly back tomorrow. I'd rather have my money back, if possible.
Assistant: Yes, of course you can. Have you brought the receipt?
Customer: I'm afraid I threw it away. I didn't know I'd need it! But your colleague will remember me.
Assistant: Well, it's always a good idea to hang on to your receipts, but we'll make an exception in your case. Here's your refund. And have a good flight back!
Customer: That's okay. And thanks!

Dialogue 2

Customer: Excuse, me. I'd like to complain about this suitcase I bought here a year ago. It's really annoying!
Assistant: Shall we go over there and talk where it's a bit quieter? I'm sure we'll be able to sort this out. So how can we help you?
Customer: While I was on holiday the lock got stuck and I had to break it open with a screwdriver. Now I can't lock the suitcase, which means I can't use it again.
Assistant: Yes, it is broken. I'm sorry you had so much trouble! Did you buy the suitcase at this branch?
Customer: Yes, I've got the receipt and the guarantee here somewhere. Just a moment … Ah, here it is.
Assistant: I see. Well, what we can do is send the suitcase to the manufacturer and have it repaired. It's still under guarantee, so you won't need to pay.
Customer: I should hope not! But what if the lock gets stuck again?
Assistant: We've never had this problem before, so I don't think it's a design fault. But if you prefer, you can exchange it for a suitcase with a different type of lock.
Customer: Actually, I quite like this particular model. I'll do what you suggest and have it repaired.
Assistant: I'm sure it won't happen again, and I'm sorry you had so much inconvenience during your holiday. Allow me to give you this leather impregnation spray to make up for it.
Customer: Oh, that's very generous of you.

a) *For each dialogue, make notes about the following points.*
- the product
- the problem
- the cause of the problem
- the proof of purchase
- the solutions suggested by the assistant
- the solution chosen by the customer

b) *How could Dialogue 2 end? Suggest further questions that the customer might ask, and how the assistant could answer them.*

Task 2 Over to you

a) *Work with a partner. Create a role play at the Customer Service Desk. Make notes about these points:*
- What item did the customer buy?
- When and where did the customer buy it?
- How much did the customer pay for it?
- Was the price already reduced?
- Is the item under guarantee?
- Does the customer have proof of purchase?
- Why is the customer not satisfied?
- What does the customer want the shop to do?

b) *Practice the role play you have created. Then swap notes with another pair and do 'their' role play.*

Useful phrases

Explaining the problem
I'm sorry to have to tell you this, but…
I bought this … here last week / a week ago.
I'm not at all satisfied because …
What are you going to do about it?
I'd prefer to have / I'd rather have …
If you don't …, then I'll …

Finding out and checking
So how can we help you?
What is it that you don't like about the product?
Could you tell me …?

Showing understanding
I see … / I understand …
So what you're saying is …
I can see why you're upset / annoyed.

Offering solutions
What we can do is give you a …
We'll exchange it for a new one.
We'll send it away for repair.
Shall I get you a …?
Would you like me to …?
If you prefer, we can …

Checking proof of purchase
Did you buy it at this branch?
Have you got the receipt?

Thanking and apologising
Thanks for telling us about it.
I'm sorry that this has happened.
I'm sorry about all the trouble you've had.
I do apologise for all the inconvenience you've had.

STEP B – In the suggestions box

Here are some cards that customers put in the 'SUGGESTIONS' box of a large supermarket.

1. I notice that your assistants who serve at the meat and fish counters don't wear gloves and they never wash their hands. Please remind them about basic rules of hygiene.

2. Although you have six checkouts, often only one of them is open – even when there are long queues.

3. Please don't put candy near the checkout. It makes it too stressful for parents with young children!

4. Why do we need to put in a Euro to get a shopping cart? We're customers, not thieves!

5. I don't think it is right to charge customers for carrier bags. Stores in other countries give them away for free, and customers use them as bin liners.

6. It would be nice to have people who could help customers pack their groceries at the checkout and then carry the bags for them to the car park.

7. Please make it easier for customers to find their way around the store, e.g. with big signs or arrows. At the moment it's like a jungle!

8. I don't like the Volkslieder you play through the loudspeakers. It would be better to play something that everyone likes.

9. Please clean the restrooms more often.

10. It would be great if your store accepted VISA and other credit cards.

11. I'd like more convenient opening hours (24/7) to make shopping easier for like me who have to work late or do night shifts.

12. Many old and disabled people aren't able to do their shopping themselves, but they can't afford to have their groceries delivered either. How about offering a free delivery service?

13. The aisles are two narrow for people with big shopping carts to pass easily. I think you should make them wider.

14. The lift is often out of order. Once I got stuck in it.

Task 1 Talking point

a) *Talk about the customers' suggestions. What do you think the store manager should do?*

b) *What should your store do to improve customer service? Note down your ideas and then ask other people in your class for their opinions.*

Useful phrases

Agreeing and disagreeing
Yes, you're right.
That's true.
Exactly!
I'm afraid I disagree.
No, I don't agree because …

Giving opinions
I think …
In my view / opinion.

Asking for opinions
Do you agree?
What do you think?
What's your opinion?
How do you feel about it?

Making suggestions
I've got a suggestion.
I think the manager should …
I suggest that the supermarket …

Task 2 Suggestions

a) *Find words in the customers' suggestions with the same meaning.*

1. things you wear on your hands to protect them
2. to tell someone not to forget something
3. people who steal things
4. to ask someone to pay for a product or service
5. place where customers pay for goods
6. things bought from a supermarket
7. something used to carry shopping
8. working from 1am – 5am, for example

b) *Use words from the text to complete the table.*

British	American
1. sweets	?
2. ?	elevator
3. shopping trolley	?
4. ?	lines (of people)
5. toilet	?
6. ?	parking lot

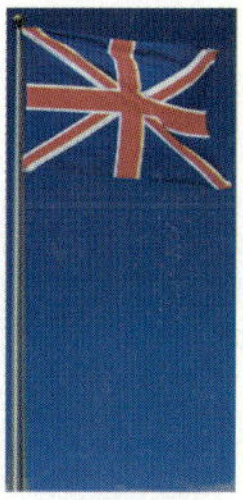

Task 3 Sounds and spelling

a) *Listen and write down the missing words.*

1. I love your new bathroom ....
2. The cornflakes are in the next ....
3. We've painted the ...... store.
4. There's a ...... in the curtain material.
5. How long have you ...... these shoes?

b) Like 'pear' and 'pair', or 'board' and 'bored', each of the missing words on the left sounds the same as another word with a different spelling. *What are the other words, and how are they spelt?*

Task 4 Customer service: Have it done by us!

Some customers don't want to do things themselves. Tell them what they can have done at this shopping centre.

Example: You can have your groceries delivered for free!

Language tip

We don't clean the shop windows ourselves. We **have** them **cleaned**.
(**Wir lassen sie putzen**.)

Task 5 Sounds and spelling: Tongue twisters

How fast can you say these tongue twisters?

Vivienne Westwood wears warm woolly vests.
Thin sinks stink and thick sticks sink.
She sells sea shells on the sea shore.

STEP C – Complaints

Task 1 Talking shop

Are the statistics on the right true of where you work?

Why do customers leave?

• They die.	1%
• They buy from friends instead.	3%
• They move away.	5%
• They are attracted by the competition's offers.	9%
• They are dissatisfied with the quality or the price.	14%
• They are dissatisfied with the customer service.	68%

Task 2 Listening: On the telephone

You will hear two conversations on the phone between customer service staff and customers.

a) *Compare the conversations.*
- Describe how each customer feels at the end of the call.
- Say which conversation you think is more successful and say why.

b) *For each conversation, make notes about the following points:*
- the product
- the problem
- the customer's name
- the product brand name
- the action taken by the assistant
- the solution agreed

c) *Listen to the second conversation and complete the sentences.*
1. This is Beate Zimmermann. How can I ...... you?
2. Oh, dear. I'm sorry to hear that. How ...... for you.

3. Yes, I .... Could I ...... your name please?
4. Well, we have plenty of them in ...... , so there won't be a problem ...... it.
5. Thank you for letting us ...... about this.
6. If you still have the ...... , that would be very ....

Task 3 Writing for work

A customer has written to DIY World to complain about a faulty product.

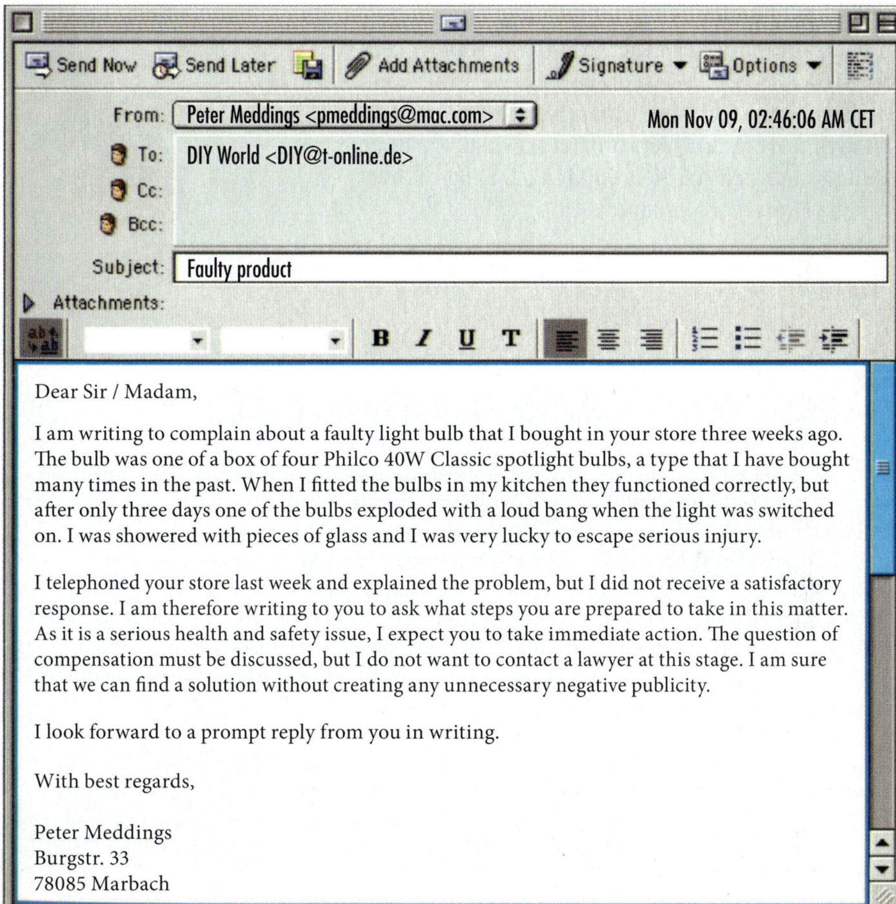
Send Now | Send Later | Add Attachments | Signature | Options

From: Peter Meddings <pmeddings@mac.com>   Mon Nov 09, 02:46:06 AM CET
To: DIY World <DIY@t-online.de>
Cc:
Bcc:
Subject: Faulty product
Attachments:

Dear Sir / Madam,

I am writing to complain about a faulty light bulb that I bought in your store three weeks ago. The bulb was one of a box of four Philco 40W Classic spotlight bulbs, a type that I have bought many times in the past. When I fitted the bulbs in my kitchen they functioned correctly, but after only three days one of the bulbs exploded with a loud bang when the light was switched on. I was showered with pieces of glass and I was very lucky to escape serious injury.

I telephoned your store last week and explained the problem, but I did not receive a satisfactory response. I am therefore writing to you to ask what steps you are prepared to take in this matter. As it is a serious health and safety issue, I expect you to take immediate action. The question of compensation must be discussed, but I do not want to contact a lawyer at this stage. I am sure that we can find a solution without creating any unnecessary negative publicity.

I look forward to a prompt reply from you in writing.

With best regards,

Peter Meddings
Burgstr. 33
78085 Marbach

Note
→ Useful phrases for letter-writing on pages 133–134.

Write a reply to the customer. The phrases below will help you.

I am very sorry that one of our products should have caused such distress, and …	We value you as a customer and hope that …	Thank you for your email of … I was naturally very concerned to hear about your alarming experience …

On receiving your email, I immediately contacted …

I also instructed the staff here in our Schwenningen store to …

I am very grateful to you for raising this important safety issue.

I am therefore enclosing a voucher for €100 which you can spend in any department of our store.

STEP D – Product recall

The Customer Service Department of the department store MORATH has received a product warning from the manufacturer of a soft toy it sells called CUDDLES. Although there are no reports of an accident, the beads pose a risk to small children, so MORATH has written this press release for a product recall.

RÜCKRUFAKTION BEZÜGLICH CUDDLES-PLÜSCHTIEREN

Hat Ihr Kind eines davon?
Bitte bringen Sie es zu Ihrem MORATH KAUFHAUS zurück.

Uns ist ein Fehler unterlaufen. Unsere Anforderungen an Kindersicherheit sind sehr streng, aber in diesem Fall hat die Qualitätskontrolle versagt. Das Stofftier CUDDLES enthält kleine Kunststoffkugeln, die aus Sicherheitsgründen in einen Innenbehälter eingenäht sind. Unglücklicherweise sind die Nähte in einigen Stofftieren nicht stabil genug, d. h., die Kügelchen können austreten. Soweit uns bekannt, ist noch kein Unfall geschehen, dennoch halten wir es für das Beste, alle CUDDLES-Stofftiere zurückzurufen. Die bloße Gefahr, dass die Nähte platzen könnten, ist Grund genug, dass Ihr Kind nicht damit spielen sollte. Kinderprodukte von MORATH sollten nicht aufplatzen.

Das Herunterschlucken der Kügelchen ist nicht gefährlich, es besteht jedoch eine gewisse Gefahr, dass das Kügelchen eingeatmet wird und in die Lunge gelangt. Sollte dies geschehen, kann es die Lungenfunktion schädigen. Aus Rücksicht auf die Kinder, bitten wir Sie, wenn Sie ein CUDDLES-Stofftier gekauft haben sollten, dieses zu MORATH zurückzubringen.

Im Austausch erhalten Sie ein anderes Stofftier oder Ihr Geld zurück. Wenn Sie das Spielzeug nicht zurückbringen können, Sie aber immer noch den Kassenbon haben, wird Ihnen das Geld zurückerstattet. Sorgen Sie aber bitte dafür, dass sich das Stofftier nicht mehr in Reichweite Ihres Kindes befindet.

Wir bedauern diesen Vorfall sehr und versichern Ihnen, dass alle Qualitäts- und Einkaufskontrollen überprüft und verbessert werden, damit dies nicht wieder geschieht.

Was Sie machen können:
Bitte bringen Sie CUDDLES zu Ihrem MORATH KAUFHAUS zurück.

Task 1 Translation

a) *Translate the press release into English. The notes below will help you.*

Notes

made mistake – children's safety standards very strict – quality checks failed contains small plastic beads sewn into inner bag – safety reasons – seams not strong enough – might burst – cause beans to come out – as far as we know, no accident has occurred – best thing is to recall CUDDLES – the risk alone is reason enough for your child not to play with it – put bead in mouth – swallow small risk – inhale – affect lung function – kindly ask – return – in exchange, get different soft toy/money back make sure – out of reach of children – regret this incident – assure you that all quality and supply measures are reviewed and improved – won't happen again

Language tip: translating

- Make sure you have a good dictionary.
- Always read the whole text before you start translating.
- Be careful with words that have different possible translations:
  Rückruf – recall (≠ call back)
- Don't translate word for word, but keep as close to the original as possible.
  Uns ist ein Fehler unterlaufen – We have made a mistake.
  Sorgen Sie aber dafür, dass ... – However, please make sure that ...
- Be careful with 'dass'
  Es besteht jedoch ein gewisse Gefahr, dass – However, there's a small risk that ... (no comma after 'that')
  Ist Grund genug, dass Ihr Kind nicht damit spielt – is reason enough for your child not to play with it
- Watch out for 'false friends':
  streng – strict (≠ strong)
  in diesem Fall – in this case (≠ in this fall)
  wenn – if (≠ when)
- Break up long German sentences. English sentences are often shorter than German ones.

b) *Translate your text (or someone else's) back into German. Then compare it with the original version in the book.*

Task 2 LEARNING SKILLS: Keeping up your English

If you don't use English every day, it can go rusty very quickly. What do you plan to do to keep up your English?

WORD POWER

Task 1 Adjectives for faulty products

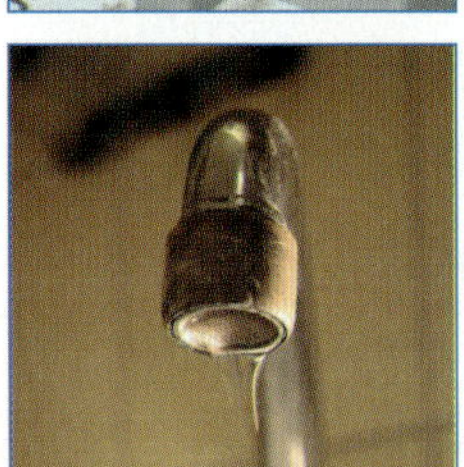
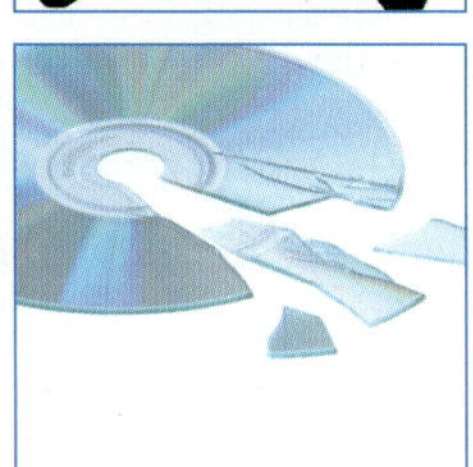
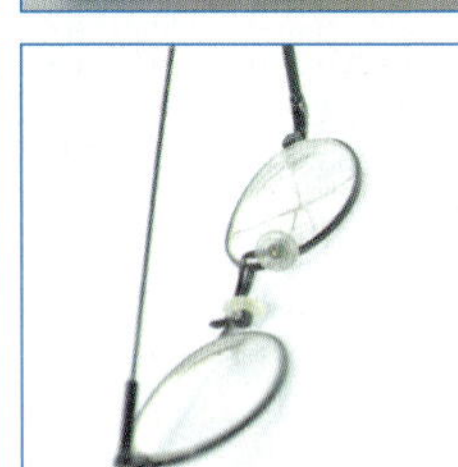
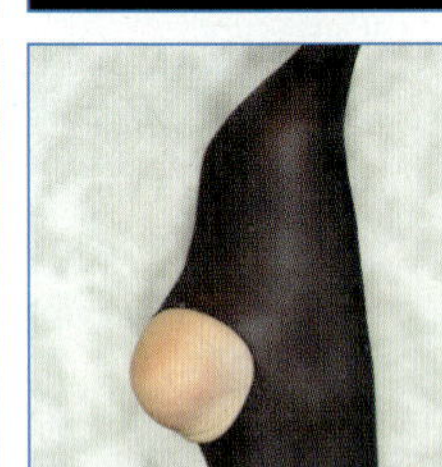

Describe what is wrong with the products in the pictures. Use words from the box below.

broken • incomplete • chipped • faded • dirty • damaged
flawed • discoloured • missing • twisted • torn • too small
scratched • bent • stained • leaking • too big • dented

Task 2 Words in context

Complete the text with the missing words.

satisfied • hygiene • refund • generous • worn • used
repaired • exchange • packaging • guarantee • complains • receipt
reduced • return • money

If a customer .... about a purchase such as an electrical appliance that is under .... or an anorak with a faulty zip in it, the shop might offer to have it .... , but this may not be possible or what the customer wants. In Germany, shops usually give customers their .... back if ....:

- the customer has got the .... as proof of purchase,
- the item has not already been .... in price,
- the item is still in its original .... ,
- the item has not yet been .... or ....

American companies have a more .... policy. For example, the mail order house Land's End tells customers: 'If you are not completely .... with any item you buy from us, at any time during your use of it, ... it and we will .... your full purchase price.' However, in both America and Germany, shops will not .... items such as lipstick and bikinis for reasons of ....

CHECK-OUT 4

A Describing products

What are the missing words?

1. user-f...
2. up-to-d...
3. an infra-r... mouse
4. high-h... shoes
5. flat-s... television
6. a gift-w... present

B False friends

Choose a better word for the false friend.

1. Our safety standards are very ~~strong~~.
2. I'll call the manager on my ~~handy~~.
3. What's your ~~meaning~~ about this?
4. I have to deal with ~~reclamations~~ in my job.
5. Have you ~~controlled~~ the receipt?
6. Please fill out this application ~~formula~~.

C German ➔ English

Translate the following expressions into English.

1. Möchten Sie eine Nachricht hinterlassen?
2. Sein Durchwahl ist 344.
3. Wir können Ihnen eine Rechnung schicken.
4. Haben Sie den Kassenbon dabei?
5. Sie können den Betrag überweisen.
6. Dieses Produkt ist für empfindliche Haut geeignet.

D The right option

Complete the sentences.

1. Do you think (*these sunglasses / this sunglass*) suit me?
2. Could you (*lend / borrow*) me your pen, please?
3. This cashmere jumper feels so (*soft / softly*).
4. The engine is very (*clever / cleverly*) designed. That's why it works so (*efficient / efficiently*).
5. How long ago (*did you buy / have you bought*) this?
6. If it (*had been / would have been*) my fault, I (*would apologise / would have apologised*).
7. (*Please, make sure, that / Please make sure that*) the product is not in the reach of children.

E Prepositions

Put in the missing prepositions

1. ...... the left
2. ...... front ...... the shop
3. to consist ......
4. a demand ...... a product
5. not ...... stock
6. a voucher €100

F Not quite the same

Explain the difference.

1. a bride and a groom
2. a recipe and a receipt
3. It suits you. / It fits you.
4. to remind someone / to remember someone
5. a flaw / a floor
6. a stained pullover / a discoloured pullover

G Useful phrases

a) *Put in the missing words.*

1. I can't afford this. It costs a f...!
2. I can't answer that. I haven't got a c...!
3. I think that we may have just the th... for you.
4. We look forward to h... from you soon.
5. What ex... do you need this product for?
6. Please accept our apologies for all the in... you have had.
7. Sorry about all the t... you've had.
8. If you have any questions, please do not h... to contact us.

b) *Which of the sentences above might you find in a formal letter?*

H Compound nouns

Match one word from each box to make a new word.

vending • after • customer lump • marital • price whole • best • ~~green~~ security	*seller • ~~grocer~~ • service status • sales • machine alarm • tag • sale • sum*

Example: greengrocer

I Lady Muck

Lady Muck is rich but helpless. Say what things she has done for her.

1. She never has to iron her bed linen herself.
2. Someone delivers her shopping in a limousine.
3. She doesn't clean her house herself, of course.
4. Someone makes her clothes for her.
5. She can't even cook her own meals.

Example: She has her bed linen ironed.

J British or American English?

a) *Is the speaker using British or American English?*

1. I'd like a burger with chips, please.
2. My car is in the parking lot.
3. The elevator is out of order.
4. I need a Euro for the shopping trolley.

b) *Give the British/American alternatives.*

K Odd one out

Which word is the odd one out?

1. pens – pencils – envelopes – tights – notepaper
2. lace – cotton – striped – wool – silk
3. turquoise – green – yellow – diamond – purple

L Accessories

Suggest an accessory that could be sold with each of these products.

1. jeans 2. paint 3. shoes 4. computer

Focus on Communication

Useful phrases with customers

Greeting	Hello. Good morning / good afternoon.	
Offering help	How can I help you? Can I help you at all? What can I do for you? I see you're looking at … / looking for … Feel free to take them off the shelf. Let me know if you need any help.	
	Would you like	to look around? (to take) a closer look? to try it on? me to show you how it works?
	If	you need any help, just let me know. I can help in any way, just ask.
Finding out the customer's needs	Are you looking for anything in particular? How are you planning to use it? Do you know what size you are? Could you tell me how you are going to use it?	
	What	sort of price do you have in mind? exactly do you need it for?
Showing you can help	*Customer:* *Assistant:* *Customer:* *Assistant:* *Customer:* *Assistant:* *Customer:* *Assistant:*	Do you speak English? Yes, a little. (OR: Yes, no problem.) Could you help me with this, please? Yes, of course. Would you mind helping me with this? No, not at all. (= You are happy to help.) Excuse me, but I have a problem. Yes, what can I do for you?
Making the customer interested	Perhaps you're interested in … How about …? Could I interest you in …? By the way, we also have a … that would go well with your … If you're looking for something versatile, then let me show you … I think that we may have just the thing for you!	
	Would you	like to try our new …? care to sample / taste one of these? like me to show you our new …?

Referring to product features	As you can see, it's a … There are / It has plenty of …	
	It is	made of … rich in …
	It	consists of contains
Describing how a product is used	It is	used by … used for (+ -ing verb) used to (+ main verb) a thing / device / tool / piece of equipment for …
	It	works like this. First you … Then you … (etc.)
Describing benefits	The material makes it … You can … This product ensures that you … The great thing is that …, which means … Because of this feature, it … There's no risk of …	
	It	helps you to … allows / enables you to …
Referring to future experience	When you …, you'll be able to … With this product, you will always …	
	You	will find that you can … won't need to worry about …
Appealing to the senses	Feel how soft it is. Doesn't it sound great? It tastes delicious. Smell this – isn't it wonderful? It looks so elegant.	

Talking about prices	It is	excellent value for money a good price. on special offer / on sale. 10% off the normal price. an offer you can't refuse.
	It	comes with a guarantee. has already been reduced by ..., which is a reduction of ...
	If you	buy two, you get one free. think it's too much to pay in one lump sum, you can always pay in instalments. It's no problem.
	You get two for the price of one. I'm afraid we can't come down on the price any more. That's the sale price. We can't reduce it further. We've dropped our prices radically. The price includes delivery and installation. Yes, the price includes sales tax / VAT.	
Talking the customer round	Yes, I see your point, but ... I understand what you're saying, but ... You're absolutely right as far as ... is concerned, but ... That's true, but on the other hand ... Exactly! But you also need to consider... That's not completely true because ...	
If the customer isn't interested	If you	need any further information, please ... can't find what you're looking for else-where, we've got plenty in stock. change your mind, we're still here.
	Let me just give you this catalogue. It's a major purchase, so I can understand that you want to think about it.	
Dealing with complaints	Could you describe what happened? What is it that you don't like about the product? I see ... / I understand ... So what you're saying is ... I can see why you're upset / annoyed. Thanks for telling us about it. We want you to be satisfied with your purchase!	
Checking proof of purchase	Did you buy it at this branch? Have you got the receipt?	

Apologising	It was	my mistake. our fault.
	I	do apologise. would like to apologise for …
	I'm very sorry	that this has happened. about this.
	Once again, please accept our apologies for any inconvenience caused.	
Offering solutions	We'll	take it back and exchange it for a new one. repair it ourselves. send it away to have it repaired.
	We can	offer you a refund. give you a voucher.
	Would you like	to choose a similar product? us to order a new one for you?
	What we can do is give you a reduction. Shall I get you a bigger size / darker colour? Since you're such a loyal customer, we would be prepared to …	
Checking satisfaction	Would that be acceptable? Is that acceptable to you? Are you happy with that?	
Responding to thanks	*Customer:* *Assistant:*	Thanks very much. You're welcome.
Responding to an apology	*Customer:* *Assistant:*	I'm very sorry. Never mind. (OR: It doesn't matter.)
Saying 'no' politely	*Customer:* *Assistant:*	Is it on sale? I'm afraid not.

Useful phrases for telephoning

Greeting	Good morning / afternoon, Megamarkt. Can I help you? What can I do for you?	
Saying who you are	Katja Schmidt speaking. This is Johannes Schweizer, from DIY World. Speaking. (response to question "Could I speak to Diana Cordes, please?")	
Checking who the caller is	Who	am I speaking to? shall I say is calling, please? is calling?
	Could I have your name, please? Is that Bettina Maier? I'm afraid I didn't catch your name.	

Getting through to the right person	Hello, Is that the Sales Department? Would you put me through to …, please?	
	Could I	speak to Carina Friedrich, please? have extension 123, please?
Putting calls through	One moment, please. I'm sorry – the line's busy / engaged. Will you wait? Please hold the line.	
	I'll	connect you with … put you through to …
Saying someone isn't available	I'm sorry, she isn't here / available at the moment. I'm afraid he isn't here today.	
Offering to take a message	Would you	like to leave a message? like me to pass on a message?
	Can I give her / him a message? Shall I ask the manager to call you back?	
Leaving messages	I'd like to leave a message for … Will you tell him / her that I called? You can tell him I'll call back later. Could you ask him to call back, please?	
Agreeing to take messages	I'll tell her as soon as she gets in. Yes, of course. I'll pass on the message.	
Saying why you're calling	It's about … (details, e.g. the customer's order) The reason I'm calling is to ask you … I need some information on … There's (a bit of) a problem with … Could you tell me … I'd like to know …	
Asking for details	Can / could you	give me your number, please? spell that for me, please?
	Right, could I have your name, please? Just a moment, I'll get a pen. OK, go ahead.	
Giving details	Have you got	something to write with? a pen handy?
Asking for time	If you	just hang on a moment, I'll … bear with me a moment, I'll just …
	Hang on, I'll just check the catalogue. I'm just accessing it on the computer. Just give me a moment to get the file. Ah yes, here it is. It's just coming up on the screen now.	

Checking that you've understood	Sorry, what was that again? Hang on, I didn't catch that. Could you repeat it? Could you just spell that word for me? Did you say thirty or thirteen? Let me just check I've got everything down correctly.
Checking that everything is clear	Would you like me to spell that for you? Have you got that? I'll just read that back to you. / I'll just spell that for you.
When the line is bad	Could you speak up a little louder, please? just speak up a bit, please? just go over that again, please?
	Sorry, it's a very bad line. I'm sorry, but we seem to have been cut off. If it happens again, I'll call you back. There seems to be someone else on the line. If you give me your number, I'll call you back.
Finishing the call	So ... is there anything else I can do for you? Well, actually, there is one more thing. (+ details) All right, we'll look into that as well. Right, well it seems as if everything is sorted out. We'll get back to you as soon as we can. Well, it was nice talking to you. Goodbye. Thank you for calling.

Hot tip

- Give telephone numbers as single digits. (Say 'two-three', NOT 'twenty-three')
- For 33 say 'double three'. For 333 say 'treble three' or 'three-double-three'.

Pronouncing letters of the alphabet

as in take		**as in tree**		**as in red**		**as in why**	**as in go**	**as in far**	**as in you**
a	h	b	c	f	l	i	o	r	q
j	k	d	e	m	n	y			u
		g	p	s	x				w
		t	v	z					

The letter 'a' rhymes with 'take'. The letter 'i' rhymes with 'why', and so on.

Hot tip

When you spell words, make sure people understand you. Say 'E' as in 'elephant', or 'i' as in 'ice cream'.

Useful phrases for letters

Referring to what you have received	Thank you (very much) for I refer to I am writing with regard to	your letter of 24th March. your order for 200 LCD monitors. your enquiry about our products.
	Further to our telephone conversation today, I would like to confirm … With regard / reference to your enquiry of 5th June, we are pleased to enclose …	
Saying why you are writing	We are writing	in connection with …
	I am writing	with reference to / with regard to … to ask you whether / to enquire about … to confirm … to let you know … / tell you that …
Giving good news	You will be glad to hear that … We are pleased to tell you that …	
Giving bad news	I am sorry to have to tell you that… I am afraid that …	
Making a request	Please … Please could / would you … We would be grateful if you could / would … I would appreciate it if you could / would …	
Offering help	If you wish, we would be happy to … Would you like us to …?	
Giving information	We would like to tell you that … We are pleased to inform you that …	
Enclosing documents	I am enclosing … / I enclose … Please find enclosed … *(letter)* Please find attached … *(e-mail)*	
Thanking	Thank you (very much) for … Many thanks for …	
Apologising	I am sorry about … We regret that this problem has happened. We apologise for any inconvenience caused. Please accept our apologies for any inconvenience you have had.	
Setting deadlines + Warning	Please ensure that the goods reach us by *(+ deadline).* We must insist on payment by *(+ deadline)* at the latest. If the goods do not reach us by *(+ deadline)*, we will *(+ action).*	

Assuring	We assure you that You can be sure that	we will do our best to put the matter right. this will not happen again.
	We promise to You can count on us to	look into the matter immediately. ensure prompt delivery in future.
Closing remarks	If you have any questions, If you require further information,	please do not hesitate to contact us. feel free to get in touch again.
Referring to future contact	We look forward to I am looking forward to	hearing from you soon / receiving your reply. meeting / seeing you next week.
	We hope to	receive your reply within the next few days.
Finishing the letter	*If you start with:* Dear Mr / Ms Bond Dear Sir or Madam	*Finish with:* Yours sincerely (BrE) / Sincerely (yours) (AmE) Yours faithfully (BrE) / Sincerely (yours) (AmE)

Sample materials

Sample Europass CV

europass **Europass curriculum vitae**	**Hot tip** Add a photograph if you think it will help you get the job
Personal information	
Name	**Markus Kammerer**
Address	Falkenweg 36, 90459 Nuremberg, Germany
Telephone	#49 (0)741 21176 Mobile: 1626346932
Email	markus_kammerer@mac.com
Nationality	German
Date of birth	17 September 1980
Desired employment	**Sales Assistant**
Work experience	
Dates	14 August 2003 – 7 July 2006
Occupation or position held	Trainee sales assistant
Main activities and responsibilities	Customer care and sales; giving advice and information Dealing with payments; issuing receipts, invoices and credit notes Stock control and checking in-coming deliveries Coding and labelling of merchandise Arranging window displays and assisting with in-store promotions Telephoning with suppliers and customers After-sales; dealing with complaints Filing and bookkeeping Written correspondence: enquiries, offers, orders Accompanying manager on visits to suppliers and trade fairs
Name and address of employer	Sport Haller Jakobstraße 23 90459 Nuremberg

For more information go to http://europass.cedefop.eu.int

Type of business or sector	Retailer of sportswear and sports equipment
Education and training	
Dates	1 September 2003 – 14 July 2006
Title of qualification awarded	*Diplom-Einzelhandelkaufmann* (diploma in retailing) *Fachhochschulreife* (advanced school-leaving certificate)
Principal subjects / Occupational skills covered	Customer-oriented selling; Presenting goods; Dealing with special sales situations; German; English; Mathematics; Bookkeeping; Science; General Studies
Name and type of organisation providing education and training	Berufsschule Robert-Würthner (vocational college)
Personal skills and competences	
Mother tongue(s)	**German**
Other language(s)	

Self-assessment	**Understanding**		**Speaking**		**Writing**
European level (*)	Listening	Reading	Spoken interaction	Spoken production	
English	B2 Independent User	B2 Independent User	B2 Independent User	B2 Independent User	B1 Independent User
French	A2 Basic User	A2 Basic User	A1 Basic User	A1 Basic User	A1 Basic User

(*) Common European Framework of Reference (CEF) level

Social skills and competences	Team leader of a children's summer camp (August 2006) Member of the Nürnberg Narrenverein (historical carnival guild)
Organisational skills and competences	Coach of under-14s football team Course speaker at college
Computer skills and competences	Microsoft, Excel and other Windows applications
Artistic skills and competences	Skilled at graphic design and photography
Other skills and competences	Certificate in first aid
Driving licence	German driving licence, Category 2
Additional information	References available on request
Annexes	Copies of certificates (*Fachhochschulreife*, Diploma)

Sample letter of application

You needn't put your name above the address.

Falkenweg 36
90450 Nürnberg
Germany

Patrick O'Connor (Manager)
Celtic Dragon
Königstr. 2
90459 Nürnberg

15th July 2006

Include a heading to show what the letter is about. This can also go below 'Dear Mr O'Connor'.

Application for the position of sales assistant

Say where you heard about the job.

Dear Mr O'Connor

I am writing to apply for the position of sales assistant in your store, as advertised in today's Nürnberger Zeitung.

Highlight points from your CV that are relevant, e.g. qualifications and work experience.

As you can see from my enclosed CV, I have recently qualified in retailing and sales as an *Einzelhandelskaufmann*. I did my apprenticeship at Sport Haller, a retailer in sportswear and equipment, and attended a day-release course at the Berufschule Robert-Würthner.

Give further information about your skills.

During this two-year period I attended regular lessons in English for sales assistants, and I have since enrolled in evening classes in Business English in order to improve my professional communication skills. Last summer I spent two weeks cycling around Ireland since I am very interested in Irish culture and folk music.

Say why you would like the job, and what you can bring to it.

The position you offer is just what I am looking for. I enjoy working with people and would also like to have a job where I can use my English and explore my interest in Celtic traditions. My knowledge of Irish folk music and my experience in selling would certainly be an asset to your store.

Refer to the next step (interview) and end with a hopeful and friendly sentence.

I would be pleased to be invited for a personal interview, and look forward to hearing from you.

Yours sincerely,

Markus Kammerer

Print your name below your signature.

Markus Kammerer

Don't forget to mention what you are sending with the letter.

Enclosed: CV and certificates

Grammar Hot Tips

Question forms

Open and closed questions

Open questions start with a question word. **Closed questions** start with a verb.

Open: How many packets would you like? I'd like four, please.
Closed: Would you like one or two packets? I'd like two, please.

Open: How can I help you? I'm looking for a present.
Closed: Can I help you? No, thanks, I'm just looking for a present.

Open questions are useful in selling because:
- customers can't say no.
- you can find out what they really want to buy or pay, and this might be more than you expect!

Examples of open questions:

When do you need it?	By the end of the week.
Why do you need this book?	To revise for tests.
Who is the present for?	My daughter's wedding.
What kind of photos do you take?	Mostly landscapes.
Which colour do you prefer?	Red.
Where is the toy department?	It's on the third floor.
How many would you like?	Three, please.
How would you like to pay?	By credit card.
How much is it?	Nine ninety-nine.
How often do you go jogging?	About twice a week.

Hot tip

- *Wo ist er?* – Where is he?
- *Wer ist er?* – Who is he?

Language tip

Cover the questions on the left so that you only see the answers. Can you remember what the questions are?

Closed questions are useful in selling if:
- you want to check information, or
- you expect or hope your customer will say 'yes'.

Here are more examples of closed questions:

Would you like to see some?	Yes, I'd love to./ No, not really.
Can I help you?	Yes, please. / No, I'm just looking.
Do you **live** in Germany?	Yes, I do. / No, I don't.
Does your son **have** a computer?	Yes, he does. / No, he doesn't.
Is he a fan of computer games?	Yes, he is. / No, he isn't.
Are you interested in them, too?	Yes, I am. / No, not at all.

Hot tip

Don't just answer 'yes' or 'no'. Repeat the verb in the answer if possible.

Asking about quantity

Use '**how many**' with things that can be counted.

- How many bottles of milk do you buy a week?

Use '**how much**' with things that cannot be counted.

- How much milk do you drink a day?

Hot tip

- How many = *Wie viele ...?*
- How much = *Wie viel ...?*

Polite questions

Asking to ask

If you want to be very polite when you ask a question, start by asking if you may ask it.

Direct	Indirect (asking to ask)
What's your address?	**May** I ask you for your address?
Give me your name.	**Would you** give me your name, please?
When do you need it?	**Could you tell me** when you need it?
Don't smoke in here.	**I'm afraid I'll have to ask you** not to smoke in here.

Hot tip

Indirect questions are very common in English. They sound more polite.

Word order

The word order in indirect questions is the same as for statements.

Direct: What **is your name**?
Indirect: May I ask what **your name is**? (NOT: ~~what is your name~~)

Direct: What **do you need** it for?
Indirect: Could you tell me what **you need** it for? (NOT: ~~what do you need~~)

I was wondering ...

Starting with 'I was wondering' also makes a question very polite.

I was wondering if I could use your phone.
I was wondering if you had the Nikon D50 in stock.
I was wondering if you would mind holding this mirror.
I was wondering if you would like to try on a smaller size.

Hot tip

Would often follows *if* in polite requests and offers.

Telling people to do things

Starting with 'would you mind' or 'do you mind' is useful when you:

- tell a customer politely to do something: **Would you mind** wait**ing** a moment?
- ask a customer politely if you can do something: **Would you mind if** I check**ed** the bill?

'Would you mind?' means 'Do you have anything against it?' so be careful with the answer.

?	☺	☹
Would you mind if I smoked?	No, not at all. Go ahead.	I'd rather you didn't.

Tenses

In the past

- I **saw** some great films last year.
- She **started** her job two weeks ago.
- When **did** you **buy** it?

Language tip

Use the **simple past** for things that happened at a time now past, when you tell a story or add details (when? where? why? who?).

Hot tip

Simple past + ago, last week/month, yesterday, at 3 o'clock, on Monday, in June, in 2005

Two events in the past

- She **left** after she **had tried on** ten pairs of shoes.
- I **felt** sick because **I'd eaten** so much chocolate.
- I **arrived** late, and the shop **had** already **closed**.

Language tip

When two events happen in the past, the **past perfect** makes it clear which of the two happened first.

Hot tip

I'd eaten = I had eaten   I'd like = I would like

Past during the past

- I **was talking** to Mrs Jones when my mobile **rang**.
- While I **was trying on** the jeans, the zip **broke**.
- I **bought** an umbrella because it **was raining**.

Language tip

Use the **past progressive** for the background, and the **simple past** for the single action or unexpected event.

Hot tip

because it was raining = *weil es (gerade) regnete*

From past to present

- I **have seen** some great films this year.
- We'**ve lived** in Munich all our lives.
- How long **have you been learning** English?

Language tip

Use the **present perfect** for things that happened or started in the past, and are important now.

Hot tip

The progressive form (have + been + ing-verb) oftenfollows 'How long ...?'

Now

- I can't talk to you now. I'**m serving** a customer.
- What **are you doing**? – **I'm trying** to open this jar!
- I think winter **is coming**. It's **getting** colder.

Language tip

Use the **present progressive** for things that are happening or changing right now, or for things that are limited in time.

Hot tip

I wear glasses *(Ich bin Brillenträger)* but I'm not wearing them now. *(Ich trage sie gerade nicht)*

As a rule

- Water **boils** at 100° centigrade.
- I usually **wear** jeans at home.
- I never **eat** breakfast.

Language tip

Use the **simple present** for routines, habits and things that are generally true.

Hot tip

('He-she-it, das 'S' muss mit.')

Plans and things 'on the way'

- What **are** you **going to do** on Saturday?
- We'**re going to go** to a football match.
- Look at those clouds. I think it'**s going to rain**.

Language tip

Use **going-to + verb** for things that have been decided, for plans and for events that you can see coming.

Hot tip

Sie bekommt ein Kind. = She's going to have a baby (NOT ~~She gets a child~~.)

Promises, warnings, offers

- This **will not happen** again, I promise.
- Be careful with that skateboard or you'**ll fall**.
- You don't need any money! I'**ll pay** for the coffee.

Language tip

Use **will + verb** for promises, warnings and offers. You can also use it for decisions that you make at the moment of speaking.

Hot tip

Ich helfe dir. = I'll help you. (NOT ~~I help you~~.)

Arrangements

- Mike and I **are playing** tennis on Sunday.
- **Are** you **meeting** Katie again this afternoon?
- I'**m going** to the doctor tomorrow.

Language tip

Use the **present progressive** for plans that have already been arranged, such as future appointments.

Hot tip

I'm going to play tennis tomorrow. *(Vorhaben)* I'm playing tennis tomorrow. *(Vereinbarung)*

If-Sentences

If can be used with different tenses, for example:

- **If** that **was** a shoplifter, why **didn't** you **stop** him?
- We'**re giving** free gifts to customers **if** they **spend** more than €500.
- **If** you **bought** this here, we'**ll exchange** it for another one.
- **If** the weather **is** good tomorrow, I'**m going** to do some gardening.

Hot tip

If the sentence starts with *if*, use a comma. You don't need one if you start with the main clause.

If you want to know what the tenses are called, see 'Grammar hot tips: tenses'

Here are the most common types of *if* sentences.

Zero conditional

- What **happens if** I **press** this button? (Or: when I press …)
- It'**s** easy **if** you **know** how. (Or: when you know how)
- **If** your mobile **rings** when you have a customer, **don't answer** it.

Language tip

If-clause
- simple present

Main clause
- simple present

1st conditional

- **If** you **like** dark chocolate, you'**ll love** these truffles!
- **If** we **have** them in stock, then we'**ll call** you.
- I'**ll buy** it elsewhere **if** you **don't give** me a better price.

Language tip

If-clause
- simple present

Main clause
- will + main verb

2nd conditional

- **If** you **bought** this in the UK, it **would cost** more.
- You **would save** electricity **if** you **used** energy-saving light bulbs.
- **If** your son **was** here, he **could try** it on himself.

Language tip

If-clause
- simple past

Main clause
- would/could + main verb

3rd conditional

- If you **had ordered** one last week, it **would have arrived** yesterday.
- If I **hadn't checked** the bill, I **wouldn't have noticed** the mistake.
- I **wouldn't have sold** it to you if I'**d known** about your allergy.

Language tip

If-clause
- had + 3rd verb from

Main clause
- would have + 3rd verb form

Hot tip

- **If** we repair it ourselves, … (possible)
- **When** people get older, … (certain)

Hot tip

Use 'then' and not 'so' in sentences with ***if***.

- ***If*** you don't call me, **then** I'll call you. (NOT: ~~so I'll call you~~)

Hot tip

Don't use 'will' or 'would' in the 'if-clause'. ***(If*** *+ would = Satz kaputt)*

- **If** you **pay** cash, we'll give you a discount. (NOT ... ~~if you will pay cash~~)
- Try on a bigger size **if** it's too small.. (NOT ... ~~if it will be too small~~)
- **If** we **reduced** our prices, our sales **would increase**. (NOT... ~~if we would reduce~~)

But: You can use 'would' in the if-clause if you want to be very polite.

- If you would come this way, please. (= Please follow me.)
- We would be pleased if you would visit our shop again.

Comparison of adjectives

short word + -er / -est

cheap → cheap**er** → the cheap**est** big → bigg**er** → the bigg**est**

- This computer is **cheaper than** the previous model.
- Our new catalogue is **bigger than** the old one.
- This is **the hottest** summer we've had for ten years.

Add -ier to short words that end in -y.
easy → eas**ier** → the eas**iest**

more / most + long word

expensive → **more** expensive → **the most** expensive

- The new mobile phones are **more expensive than** the old models.
- I think this year's product range is **more interesting than** last year's.
- The hard disk drive is **the most important** part of the computer.

irregular forms

good → better → (the) best bad → worse → (the) worst far → further → (the) furthest

- It's a long way to the airport. It's **further than** I thought.
- We hope that next month's sales will be **better than** this month's.
- That was **the worst** customer I've ever met!

(not) as ... as

Use as ... as, or not as ... as to show how things are the same or different.

- The canvas bag is **as big as** the leather one and it is **just as strong**.
- The leather bag is not **as light as** the canvas bag.
- No-name products are often just **as good as** the well-known brands, but **not as expensive**.

Hot tip

schneller als = faster **than** (NOT: ~~faster as~~)
so groß wie = as big as (NOT: ~~so big as~~)

Hot tip

the most popular product **in** the shop (NOT: ~~of~~)

Prepositions of time

on

• days of the week	Are you open **on Sunday**?
• dates	Our new store opens **on 14th October**.

Hot tip

We say: on **the** fourteenth **of** October.

in

• parts of the day	I'll collect it **in the morning**. I don't work **in the afternoon**. We'll meet them for dinner **in the evening**. We felt an earthquake **in the night**.
• months	My birthday is **in June**. The new model will be launched **in September**.
• seasons	We sell most of our warm coats **in autumn**.
• years	The shopping centre was opened **in 2006**.

Hot tip

You can also say: in **the** autumn AmE: in **(the)** fall

at

• times of the clock	Our launch party will start **at 17.30**. I'll meet you **at 3 o'clock**.
• times of day	We can discuss the problem **at lunchtime**. Our automatic heating system switches off **at night**.
• festivals and public holidays	The roads are always busy **at Christmas time**. We sell a lot of chocolate bunnies **at Easter**.

Hot tip

We write: 17.30 5pm **We say**: five-thirty five o'clock

over

- during a fixed period — We'll be closed **over** the summer.
  The goods will arrive **over** the next few days.

Hot tip

over is like 'during'

by

- deadlines — We must finish the window display **by 9 o'clock**.
  The invoice must be paid **by 15th June**.

until

- point when something stops — On Thursdays we stay open **until 9 o'clock**.
  The offer is open **until 15th June**.

Hot tip

by = no later than **until** = going on up to

Countable and uncountable nouns

countable nouns	uncountable nouns
a lot of/lots of (large number) *Example* • I've eaten **lots of** Easter eggs. • In fact, I've eaten too **many** eggs.	**a lot of / lots of** (large amount) *Example* • I've eaten **lots of** chocolate. • In fact, I've eaten too **much** chocolate.
a few (a small number) *Example* • I'll have **a few carrots**.	**a little** (a small amount) *Example* • I only want **a little rice**.

Uncountable in English

countable in German	uncountable in English.	typical mistake
Ich habe einige Informationen für Sie.	I have some **information** for you.	NOT: ~~some informations~~
Ich gebe Ihnen ein Rat.	I'll give you some **advice**. I'll give you a piece of **advice**.	NOT: ~~an advice~~
Gute Kenntnisse der englischen Sprache sind erforderlich.	A good **knowledge** of English is necessary.	NOT: ~~knowledges in English language~~
Sie haben eine gute Arbeit geleistet.	You've done good **work**/a good job.	NOT: ~~a good work~~.

countable in German	uncountable in English.	typical mistake
Ich habe eine gute Nachricht für Sie.	I have some good **news** for you.	NOT: ~~a good news~~
Wann kommen die Nachrichten?	When is the **news**?	NOT: ~~are the news~~
Ich habe viele Erfahrungen im Einzelhandel.	I have a lot of **experience** in retailing.	NOT: ~~experiences~~
Seine Haare werden grau.	His **hair** is going grey.	NOT: ~~are going grey~~.

Learning tip

Collect more examples of uncountable nouns, e.g. furniture, equipment, luggage, bread, spaghetti

Plural form in English

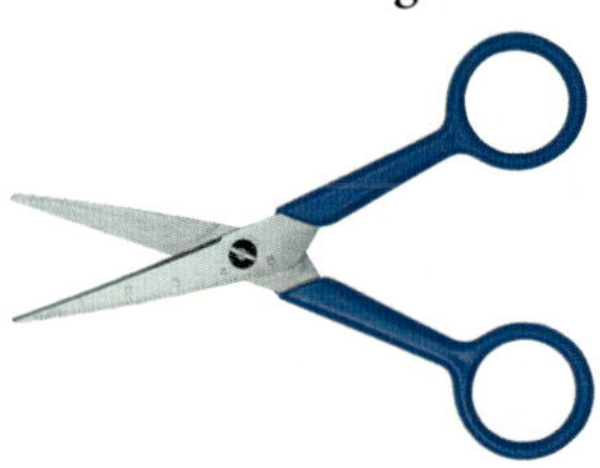

(a pair of) scissors

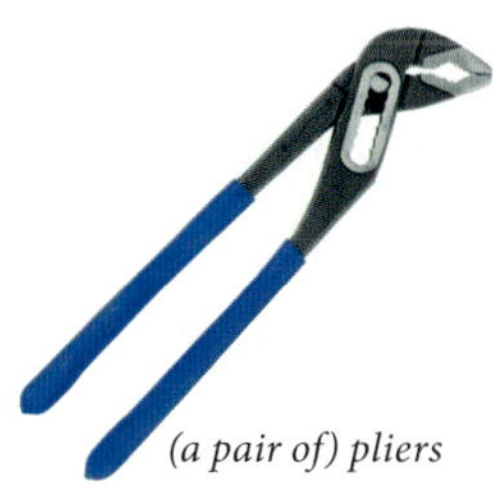

(a pair of) pliers

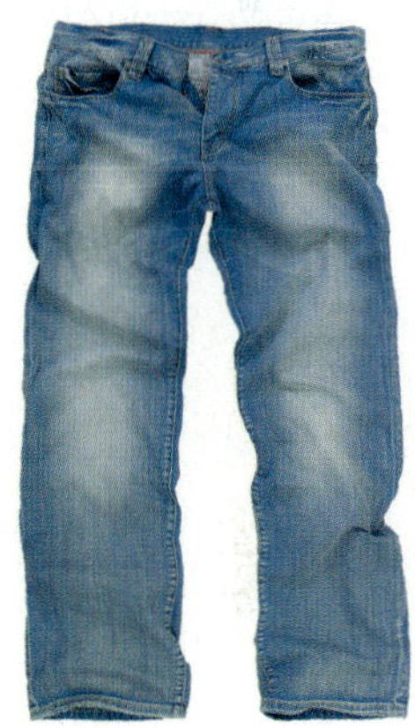

(a pair of) trousers

(a pair of) shorts

Hot tip

Remember the plural form: The scissors **are** sharp. (NOT: ~~The scissor is sharp~~)

Common mistakes in speaking

Here are some common mistakes that learners make when speaking English, with corrections and tips.

wrong tense / verb form	right tense	tip
I have seen him yesterday. When have you bought it?	I **saw** him yesterday. When **did you buy** it?	Use the simple past for things that happened in a time now over.
How long do you live in Munich? I live here for three years.	How long **have you lived** in Munich? I have lived here for three years.	Use the present perfect with 'how long', 'since' and 'for'.
I think winter comes. It gets colder.	I think winter **is coming**. It's **getting colder**.	Present progressive for current trends and developments.
We go to a trade fair tomorrow.	We'**re going** to a trade fair tomorrow.	Present progressive for future arrangements. ('We're going to go' is also possible if this is a plan.)
I can't talk to you now. I serve a customer.	I'**m serving** a customer.	Present progressive for things happening only at the moment.
I help you.	I'**ll help** you.	Use the 'will-future' with offers of help.
He live in Düsseldorf.	He **lives** in Düsseldorf.	After he / she / it, regular verbs in the present tense have an 's'.
The glass would break if you would drop it.	The glass would break if you **dropped** it.	No 'will' or 'would' after 'if' (exception: polite request)

wrong sentence structure	right structure	tip
Do you want that we send it?	Do you **want us to** send it?	Don't use 'that' after 'want' or 'would like'
I suggest you to write a letter.	I suggest **that you** write a letter. (Or: I suggest **writing** a letter.)	Only use the 'ing' form if it is clear who the suggestion is for.
I eat always breakfast.	I **always eat** breakfast.	Adverbs of frequency *(Häufigkeit)* come before the verb. (Exception: modal verbs and forms of 'to be'.)

word missing / not necessary	the right word(s)	tip
It will come in the next days.	It will come in the **next few days**.	the next few / the last few hours / days / weeks / years
I'm sales assistant.	I'm **a** sales assistant.	Use indefinite articles ('a' / 'an') with job titles. (Exception: I'm assistant to the Store Manager.)
Shall we meet us for lunch?	Shall we **meet for lunch**?	'Meet' (like 'decide', 'concentrate', 'remember', 'sit', 'imagine', 'feel') are not reflexive in English.
Let's discuss about the problem in the office.	Let's **discuss the problem** in the office.	to discuss something to have a discussion about something

wrong word(s) / word form	the right word(s)	tip
Do you like something to drink?	**Would you** like something to drink?	Do you like = *Mögen Sie ...?* Would you like = *Möchten Sie?*
Have you made your homework?	Have you **done** your homework?	'do' with activities, e.g. shopping, cleaning, cooking, housework, homework.
I bought this scarf for two days.	I bought this scarf two days **ago**.	for two weeks = *zwei Wochen lang* two weeks ago = *vor zwei Wochen*
That colour really fits you.	That colour really **suits** you.	It fits you. = *Es passt von der Größe.* It suits you = *Es steht Ihnen gut.*
I have some informations for you. He gave me a good advice.	I have **some information** for you. He gave me **some good advice**. (or: **a good piece of advice**.)	'Information' and 'advice' are uncountable in English. Here are more examples: furniture, work (in the sense of *Arbeit*), equipment, trousers, luggage, spaghetti.
You mustn't buy batteries. They're included.	You **don't have to** (or: **needn't**) buy batteries.	You mustn't = *Sie dürfen nicht.*
You must pay VAT.	You **have to** pay VAT. (Or: You need to...)	You must = *Ich befehle Ihnen* You have to / need to = *Man muss*

You have the possibility to pay by credit card.	You **can pay** by credit card. You **have the option of paying** by credit card. **It is possible (for you) to pay** by credit card.	Have' and 'possibility' do not usually go together.
He told that it is out of stock.	He **said** that it is out of stock. He **told me** that it is out of stock.	to say something to tell someone something
Could you borrow me your pen please?	Could you lend me your pen, please? Could I borrow your pen, please?	lend to someone (like 'give') borrow from someone (like 'take')
I've been learning Spanish since six months.	I've been learning Spanish **for six months.** / I've been learning Spanish **since January**.	for + period of time since + point in time
– Would you like another drink? – Thank you.	**No, thank you.**	No, thank you. (= You refuse.) Yes, please. (= You accept.)
You can borrow it, but I need it back until Monday.	You can borrow it, but I need it back **by** Monday.	Use 'by' with deadlines. until = going on up to by = no later than
I work by Mediamarkt.	I work **for / at** Mediamarkt.	to work for an employer to work at a place
We offer these to a price of €45.99.	We offer these **at** a price of €45.99.	Use 'at' with price and cost
When you buy two, you will get one free.	**If** you buy two, you will get one free.	The German '*wenn*' is normally translated as 'if' in English.

You can find more about 'false friends' such as 'when' / 'wenn' on pages 189–191.

Vocabulary

Unit based vocabulary

Unit 1 – First contacts

working hours	[ˌwɜːkɪŋ 'aʊəz]	Arbeitszeit, Arbeitsstunden
shop (AE: **store**)	[ʃɒp]; [stɔːr]	Laden, Geschäft
customer	['kʌstəmə]	Kunde, Kundin
task	[tɑːsk]	Aufgabe
to **sell**	[sel]	verkaufen
to **deal with**	[diːl wɪð]	zu tun haben mit, umgehen mit
to **work**	[wɜːk]	arbeiten
retailing	['riːteɪlɪŋ]	Einzelhandel
branch	[brɑːntʃ]	Filiale, Zweigstelle
to **be located**	[biː ləʊ'keɪtɪd]	liegen, sich befinden
in charge of	[ɪn tʃɑːdʒ əv]	zuständig
responsible for	[rɪ'spɒnsəbl fɔː]	verantwortlich für, zuständig für
to **make a sale**	[ˌmeɪkə'seɪl]	einen Verkaufsabschluss tätigen
to **buy**	[baɪ]	kaufen
purchase	['pɜːtʃəs]	Kauf
to **purchase**	['pɜːtʃəs]	kaufen
checkout	['tʃekaʊt]	Kasse
cash desk	[kæʃ desk]	Kasse
to **show**	[ʃəʊ]	zeigen
to **demonstrate**	['demənstreɪt]	vorführen, demonstrieren
to **complain (about)**	[kəm'pleɪn ə'baʊt]	reklamieren, sich beschweren über
to **pay for**	[peɪ fɔː]	zahlen, bezahlen
department store	[dɪ'pɑːtmənt ˌstɔː]	Kaufhaus
shopping centre (BE)	['ʃɒpɪŋ ˌsentə]	Einkaufszentrum
shopping mall (AE)	['ʃɒpɪŋ ˌmɔːl]	Einkaufszentrum
sales assistant	['seɪlz ə'sɪstənt]	Verkaufsassistent/in, Verkäufer/in
to **compare**	[kəm'peə]	vergleichen
to **prepare**	[prɪ'peə]	vorbereiten

curriculum vitae (AE: **résumé**)	[kəˌrɪkjələm 'viːtaɪ]; ['rezʊmeɪ]	Lebenslauf
letter of application	['letər əv ˌæplɪ'keɪʃən]	Bewerbungsschreiben
suburb	['sʌbɜːb]	Vorort
equipment	[ɪ'kwɪpmənt]	Geräte, Ausstattung
work experience	['wɜːk ɪkˌspɪəriəns]	Arbeitserfahrung
business magazine	['bɪznəs ˌmægə'ziːn]	Wirtschaftsjournal
main store	['meɪn ˌstɔː]	Hauptgeschäft
impression	[ɪm'preʃən]	Eindruck
support	[sə'pɔːt]	Unterstützung
colleague	['kɒliːg]	Mitarbeiter/in, Kolleg/in
working environment	['wɜːkɪŋ ɪnˌvaɪrənmənt]	Arbeitsklima
to **attend college**	[ə'tend 'kɒlɪdʒ]	die (Berufs)Schule besuchen
office	['ɒfɪs]	Büro
boring	['bɔːrɪŋ]	langweilig
item	['aɪtəm]	Gegenstand, Ware
Do-it-Yourself (DIY)	[duː ɪt jɔː'self]; [diː aɪ waɪ]	(selber machen =) Baumarkt
pet	[pet]	Haustier
toy	[tɔɪ]	Spielzeug
cycle	[saɪkl]	Fahrad
furniture	['fɜːnɪtʃə]	Möbel
household goods	['haʊshəʊld gʊdz]	Haushaltswaren
ladies' fashion	['leɪdiːz 'fæʃən]	Damenmode
leisure clothing	['leʒə 'kləʊðɪŋ]	Freizeitskleidung
textiles	['tekstaɪlz]	Textilien
furnishings	['fɜːnɪʃɪŋz]	Inneneinrichtung
home entertainment	[həʊm ˌentə'teɪnmənt]	Unterhaltungselektronik
electrical goods	[ɪ'lektrɪkəl gʊdz]	Elektrowaren
basement	['beɪsmənt]	Untergeschoss
ground floor	[graʊnd flɔː]	Erdgeschoss
Excuse me	[ɪk'skjuːz mi]	Entschuldigen Sie bitte
earrings	['ɪərɪŋz]	Ohrringe
ham	[hæm]	Schinken
boots	[buːts]	Stiefel
tights	[taɪts]	Strumpfhose
paint	[peɪnt]	Farbe
peas	[piːz]	Erbsen
envelopes	['envələʊps]	Briefumschläge

sweets (AE: candy)	[swiːts]; ['kændi]	Süßigkeiten, Konfekt, Naschereien
toothpaste	['tuːθpeɪst]	Zahnpaste
potatoes	[pə'teɪtəʊz]	Kartoffeln
trousers	['traʊzəz]	Hose
matches	['mætʃɪz]	Streichhölzer
stationer/ stationer's/ stationers	['steɪʃənə], [-z]	Schreibwarengeschäft
butcher	['bʊtʃə]	Metzger, Metzgerei
greengrocer	['griːnˌgrəʊsə]	Obst- und Gemüsehändler, Lebensmittelhändler
newsagents	['njuːzˌeɪdʒənts]	Zeitungs- und Tabakhändler
vending machine	['vendɪŋ məˌʃiːn]	Automat
boutique	[buː'tiːk]	(kleines) Modegeschäft
success	[sək'ses]	Erfolg
advice	[əd'vaɪs]	Rat, Ratschlag
chemists/ chemist's/ chemist	['kemɪsts]; ['kemɪst]	Apotheke, Pharmacie, Drogerie
shelf (**pl. shelves**)	[ʃelf]; [ʃelvz]	Regal
price tag	['praɪs ˌtæg]	Preisetikett
to **give** sth. **as a present**	[gɪv 'sʌmθɪŋ æz ə 'preszənt]	schenken, etwas als Geschenk geben
blanket	['blæŋkɪt]	Decke
biscuits	['bɪskwɪts]	Kekse
receipt	[rɪ'siːt]	Beleg, Quitting, Kassenbon
for free	[fə friː]	kostenlos
plaster	['plɑːstə]	Wundpflaster
to **put** s.o. **through**	[pʊt 'sʌmwʌn θruː]	jd. durchstellen
extension	[ɪk'stenʃən]	Durchwahl
You're welcome.	[jʊə 'welkəm]	Bitte schön. (Antwort auf 'Danke')
Never mind.	['nevə maɪnd]	Das macht nichts.
I can manage.	[aɪ kən 'mænɪdʒ]	Ich schaffe es.
boutique	[buː'tiːk]	(kleines) Modegeschäft
to **sneeze**	[sniːz]	niesen
Bless you.	['bles ˌju]	Gesundheit.
Would you mind....?	[wʊd ju maɪnd]	Macht es Ihnen etwas aus?
No, not at all.	[nəʊ nɒt ət ɔːl]	Nein, überhaupt nicht.

Vocabulary

I'm afraid…	[aɪm ə'freɪd]	leider
to **offer**	['ɒfə]	anbieten
Here you are. (AE: **Here you go.**)	[hɪə ju ɑː]; [hɪr ju goʊ]	Bitte schön. (beim Geben)
note (AE: **bill**)	[nəʊt]; [bɪl]	Geldschein
change	[tʃeɪndʒ]	Wechselgeld
directions	[dɪ'rekʃənz]; [daɪ-]	Wegbeschreibungen, Wegweiser, Richtungen
opposite	['ɒpəzɪt]	gegenüber
straight ahead	[streɪt ə'hed]	geradeaus
to **turn**	[tɜːn]	drehen, wenden
next to	['nekst ˌtu]	neben
escalator	['eskəleɪtə]	Rolltreppe
frying pan	['fraɪɪŋˌ pæn]	Bratpfanne
lift	[lɪft]	Aufzug
main entrance	['meɪn ˌentrəns]	Haupteingang
gift	[gɪft]	Geschenk
mobile phone (AE: cell phone)	[ˌməʊbaɪl 'fəʊn]; [sel foʊn]	Handy
gents	[dʒents]	Männertoilette
footwear	['fʊtweə]	Schuhware
white goods (= **household appliances**)	['waɪt ˌgʊdz]; ['haʊshəʊld ə'plaɪənsɪz]	Weißware, Haushaltsgeräte
range	[reɪndʒ]	Sortiment
dishwasher	['dɪʃwɒʃə]	Spülmaschine
freezer	['friːzə]	Gefrierkammer, Tiefkühlschrank
washing-machine, washing machine	['wɒʃɪŋ məˌʃiːn]	Waschmaschine
photocopier	['fəʊtəʊˌkɒpiə]	Kopiergerät
to **introduce oneself**	[ˌɪntrə'djuːs wʌnˌself]	sich vorstellen
audience	['ɔːdiəns]	Zuschauer, Zuhörer
workspace	['wɜːkspeɪs]	Arbeitsplatz, Arbeitsbereich
enquiry	[ɪn'kwaɪəri]; [ɪŋ-]	Anfrage
retail outlet	[ˌriːteɪl 'aʊtlet]	Verkaufsstelle
details	['diːteɪlz]	Einzelheiten
payment	['peɪmənt]	Zahlung
delivery	[dɪ'lɪvəri]	Lieferung
to **look forward to**	[lʊk 'fɔːwəd tu]	sich auf etwas freuen

to **receive**	[rɪ'siːv]	erhalten, bekommen
after-sales	['ɑːftəˌseɪlz]	Kundendienst
apprentice	[ə'prentɪs]	Lehrling
apprenticeship	[ə'prentɪsʃɪp]	Lehre
brand	[brænd]	Markenname
to **tidy**	['taɪdi]	aufräumen
price tag	['praɪs ˌtæg]	Preisetikett
to **stack**	[stæk]	stapeln, sammeln
shelf (pl. **shelves**)	[ʃelf]; [ʃelvz]	Regal
supplier	[sə'plaɪə]	Lieferant, Zulieferer
scissors	['sɪzəz]	Schere

Vocabulary

Unit 2 – Products and Services

impractical	[ɪm'præktɪkəl]	unpraktisch
ugly	['ʌgli]	hässlich
up-to-date	[ˌʌptə'deɪt]	aktuell
convenient	[kən'viːniənt]	bequem, gelegen, praktisch
inexpensive	[ˌɪnɪk'spensɪv]	(vom Preis) erschwinglich
stylish	['staɪlɪʃ]	schick
faulty	['fɔːlti]	defekt, fehlerhaft
disappointing	[ˌdɪsə'pɔɪntɪŋ]	enttäuschend
versatile	['vɜːsətaɪl]	vielseitig, wendig
old-fashioned	[ˌəʊld'fæʃənd]	altmodisch
unreliable	[ˌʌnrɪ'laɪəbl]	unzuverlässig
inefficient	[ˌɪnɪ'fɪʃənt]	ineffizient, unrentabel, unwirtschaftlich
healthy	['helθi]	gesund
trainers (AE: **sneakers**)	['treɪnəz]; ['sniːkəz]	Turnschuhe
ski-jacket	['skiːˌdʒækɪt]	Skijacke
to **fold**	[fəʊld]	falten
to **agree**	[ə'griː]	(hier) einig sein, der gleicher Meinung sein
value for money	['væljuː fə 'mʌni]	gutes Preis-Leistungs-Verhältnis
reasonably priced	['riːzənəbli praɪst]	erschwinglich, einen vernünftigen Preis haben
competitive	[kəm'petɪtɪv]	wettbewerbsfähig, konkurrenzfähig

reputation	[ˌrepjə'teɪʃən]	Ruf
to **stand for** sth.	[stænd fɔː]	für etwas stehen, einen Namen haben für etwas
market leader	['mɑːkɪt 'liːdə]	Marktführer
fashionable	['fæʃənəbl]	modisch
to **be 'in'**, to **be 'the latest in'**	[bi ɪn]; [bi ðə 'leɪtɪst ɪn]	die letzte Schrei sein
sophisticated	[sə'fɪstɪkeɪtɪd]	komplex, raffiniert, ausgeklügelt
state-of-the-art	[steɪt əv ði ɑːt]	Stand der Technik
well-made	[ˌwel'meɪd]	gut gebaut
durable	['djʊərəbl]	haltbar, langlebig
economical	[ˌiːkə'nɒmɪkəl]	wirtschaftlich, effizient
user-friendly	[ˌjuːzə'frendli]	nutzerfreundlich
comfort	['kʌmfət]	Komfort, Gemütlichkeit
comfortable	['kʌmfətəbl]	bequem, angenehm, gemütlich
convenience	[kən'viːniəns]	Bequemlichkeit, Annehmlichkeit, Vorteil, Nutzen
product range	['prɒdʌkt ˌreɪndʒ]	Produktpalette, Produktsortiment
product line	['prɒdʌkt ˌlaɪn]	Produktlinie
advantage	[əd'vɑːntɪdʒ]	Vorteil
disadvantage	[ˌdɪsəd'vɑːntɪdʒ]	Nachteil
no-name brand	[ˌnəʊ 'neɪm 'brænd]	Eigenmarke, No-Name-Produkt
flyer	['flaɪə]	Flugblatt, Prospekt
silk	[sɪlk]	Seide
scarf	[skɑːf]	Schal, Halstuch
fragrance	['freɪgrəns]	Duft, Parfum
to **introduce** so. to so.	[ˌɪntrə'djuːs ˌsʌmwʌn tʊ ˌsʌmwʌn]	jmdn. jmdn. bekanntmachen
authentic	[ɔː'θentɪk]	authentisch, echt
suede	[sweɪd]	Wildleder
gloves	[glʌvz]	Handschuhe
handbag	['hændbæg]	Handtasche
wireless	['waɪələs]	drahtlos, schnurlos
accessory	[ək'sesəri]	Accessoire, Zubehör
leather case	['leðə ˌkeɪs]	Lederetui
stainless-steel	[ˌsteɪnləs 'stiːl]	Edelstahl

diver	['daɪvə]	Taucher
watch	[wɒtʃ]	Armbanduhr
waterproof	['wɔːtəpruːf]	wasserfest
cordless	['kɔːdləs]	kabelfrei, schnurlos
attachment	[ə'tætʃmənt]	Zubehör, Ansatzstück, Zusatzgerät
carved	['kɑːvd]	geschnitzt
chess set	[tʃes set]	Schachspiel
hand-made	['hændmeɪd]	handgearbeitet, handgefertigt
craftsman	['krɑːftsmən]	Kunsthandwerker
spicy	['spaɪsi]	würzig
colourful	['kʌləfʊl]	bunt
delicious	[dɪ'lɪʃəs]	lecker, wohlschmeckend
selection	[sɪ'lekʃən]	Auswahl
basket	['bɑːskɪt]	Korb
rough	[rʌf]	(hier) struppig, kraus
air balloon	['eə bəˌluːn]	(Heiß-)Luftballon
gas burner	['gæs ˌbɜːnə]	Gasbrenner
unicycle	['juːnɪˌsaɪkl]	Einrad
instructions	[ɪn'strʌkʃənz]	Anweisungen
space	[speɪs]	(hier) Weltall, Luftraum
enamelling kit	[ɪ'næməlɪŋ ˌkɪt]	Kit für Emailmalerei
badge	[bædʒ]	Lederetui
scent	[sent]	Duft, Parfum
cookie (BE: biscuit)	['kʊki]; ['bɪskwɪt]	Keks
genuine	['dʒenjuɪn]	echt
tasty	['teɪsti]	lecker, schmackhaft
artificial	[ˌɑːtɪ'fɪʃəl]	künstlich
smooth	[smuːð]	glatt, eben
out-of-date	[ˌaʊt əv 'deɪt]	altmodisch, abgelaufen, veraltet
tough	[tʌf]	hart, robust
silver	['sɪlvə]	Silber, silber
to **serve**	[sɜːv]	bedienen
Are you being served?	[ɑː ju 'biːɪŋ sɜːvd]	Werden Sie schon bedient?
cuckoo-clock	['kʊkuː ˌklɒk]	Kuckucksuhr
actually	['æktʃuəli]	eigentlich
to **originate from**	[ə'rɪdʒəneɪt frɒm]	stammen aus

to **prefer**	[prɪ'fɜː]	vorziehen
plastic	['plæstɪk]	Kunststoff
hunting gun	['hʌntɪŋ ˌgʌn]	Jagdgewehr
to **decide**	[dɪ'saɪd]	sich entscheiden
flat	[flæt]	flach
fabric	['fæbrɪk]	Stoff, Gewebe, Textilien
lace	[leɪs]	Spitze
fibres	['faɪbəz]	Fasern
pattern	['pætən]	Muster, Design
check	[tʃek]	kariert
gem	[dʒem]	Edelstein
aluminium (AE: **aluminum**)	[ˌæljə'mɪniəm]; [ə'luːmɪnəm]	Alu
sapphire	['sæfaɪə]	Saphir
striped	[straɪpt]	mit Streifen, gestreift
emerald	['emərəld]	Smaragd
cotton	['kɒtən]	Baumwolle
iron	['aɪən]	Eisen
diamond	['daɪəmənd]	Diamant
turquoise	['tɜːkwɑːz]	Türkis
polka dot	['pɒlkə ˌdɒt]	Tupfen, Pünktchenmuster
portable	['pɔːtəbl]	tragbar
light	[laɪt]	leicht
to **weigh**	[weɪ]	wiegen
to **consist of**	[kən'sɪst əv]	bestehen aus
handset	['hændset]	Telefonhörer
attached to	[ə'tætʃt tu]	verbunden mit, befestigt an
device	[dɪ'vaɪs]	(kleines) Gerät
to **record**	[rɪ'kɔːd]	aufnehmen
recording	[rɪ'kɔːdɪŋ]	Aufnahme
cable	[keɪbl]	Kabel
wire	['waɪə]	Schnur, Draht, Kabel
to **assemble**	[ə'sembl]	montieren, zusammenbauen
tool	[tuːl]	Werkzeug, Mittel
tiny	['taɪni]	winzig
announcement	[ə'naʊnsmənt]	Ansage, Durchsage, Bekannmachung

sale	[seɪl]	Schlussverkauf, Aktion mit Sonderangebote
tiny	['taɪni]	winzig
equipment	[ɪ'kwɪpmənt]	Ausrüstung, Ausstattung, Geräte
accessories	[ək'sesəriz]	Zubehör
downhill skiing	[ˌdaʊnhɪl 'skiːɪŋ]	Abfahrtskifahren, Alpinskifahren
cross-country skiing	[ˌkrɒskʌntri 'skiːɪŋ]	Langlaufskifahren
climber	['klaɪmə]	Bergsteiger
hiker	['haɪkə]	Wanderer
to **choose**	[tʃːuz]	wählen
kitchenware	['kɪtʃənweə]	Küchenuntensilien
saucepan	['sɔːspæn]	Kochtopf
kitchen appliance	['kɪtʃən ə'plaɪəns]	Kuchengerät
microwave	['maɪkrəʊweɪv]	Mikrowellenherd
kettle	[ketl]	Wasserkocher, Kessel
coffee-maker	['kɒfiˌmeɪkə]	Kaffeemaschine
available	[ə'veɪləbl]	erhältlich
to **miss**	[mɪs]	verpassen
plenty	['plenti]	viel, eine Menge
brand new	[brænd njuː]	nagelneu
to **browse**	[braʊz]	schmökern
staff	[stɑːf]	Personal
to **advise**	[əd'vaɪz]	beraten
screen	[skriːn]	Bildschirm
selection	[sɪ'lekʃən]	Auswahl
attention	[ə'tenʃən]	Aufmerksamkeit
announcement	[ə'naʊnsmənt]	Ansage, Durchsage
reduced	[rɪ'djuːst]	reduziert
on sale	[ɒn seɪl]	im Angebot
base	[beɪs]	Boden
to **light**	[laɪt]	anzünden
candle	[kændl]	Kerze
angel	['eɪndʒəl]	Engel
to **rotate**	[rəʊ'teɪt]	Ansage, Durchsage, Bekannmachung
to **fit**	[fɪt]	anbringen, montieren
to **strike**	[straɪk]	schlagen

bell	[bel]	Glocke
shape	[ʃeɪp]	Form
to **stand**	[stænd]	stellen, legen
demonstration	[ˌdemən'streɪʃən]	Vorführung
beans	[biːnz]	Bohnen
to **plug in**	[ˌplʌg 'ɪn]	einstecken
to **switch on** (= to turn on)	[ˌswɪtʃ 'ɒn]; [ˌtɜːn 'ɒn]	anschalten
to **switch off** (= to turn off)	[ˌswɪtʃ 'ɒf]; [ˌtɜːn 'ɒf]	ausschalten
to **press**	[pres]	drücken
to **warm up**	[ˌwɔːm 'ʌp]	aufwärmen
button	['bʌtən]	Knopf
noisy	['nɔɪzi]	laut
to **drop**	[drɒp]	fallen lassen
strap	[stræp]	Armband
wrist	[rɪst]	Handgelenk
shutter	['ʃʌtə]	Verschluss
screen	[skriːn]	Display, Schirm
to **store**	[stɔː]	speichern
memory stick	['meməri ˌstɪk]	USB-Stick, Datenträger
ski pole	['skiːpəʊl]	Skistock
ski goggles	['skiː ˌgɒglz]	Skibrille
to **compete with**	[kəm'piːt wɪð]	konkurrieren mit
competition	[ˌkɒmpə'tɪʃən]	Konkurrenz, Wettbewerb
competitor	[kəm'petɪtə]	Konkurrent
wasteful	['weɪstfʊl]	verschwenderisch
to **sell like hot cakes**	[ˌsel laɪk ˌhɒt 'keɪks]	wie warme Semmeln verkaufen lassen
to **do an apprenticeship**	[du ən ə'prentɪsʃɪp]	eine Lehre machen
queue	[kjuː]	Schlange
to **queue up** (AE: to stand in line)	[ˌkjuː 'ʌp]; [stænd ɪn laɪn]	Schlange stehen
umbrella	[ʌm'brelə]	Regenschirm
to **promise**	['prɒmɪs]	versprechen
light bulb	['laɪt ˌbʌlb]	Glühbirne
supervisor	['suːpəvaɪzə]	Betreuer, Ausbildungsleiter
to **have a day off**	[hæv ə deɪ ɒf]	ein Tag frei haben
tableware	['teɪblweə]	Tischgeschirr
stationery	['steɪʃənəri]	Schreibwaren, Bürobedarf

detergent, detergents	[dɪ'tɜːdʒənt]; [-s]	Waschmittel
fabric softener	['fæbrɪk ˌsɒfənə]	Weichspüler
chest of drawers	[ˌtʃest əv 'drɔːz]	Kommode
tennis racket	['tenɪs ˌrækɪt]	Tennisschläger
bowl	[bəʊl]	Schüssel, Schale
paper jam	['peɪpə ˌdʒæm]	Papierstau

Unit 3 – Customers

to **make up one's mind**	[meɪk ʌp wʌnz maɪnd]	entscheiden, sich entschließen
to **treat**	[triːt]	behandeln
to **spend** (money)	[spend] (['mʌni])	(Geld) ausgeben
to **stay within one's budget**	[steɪ wɪ'ðɪn wʌnz 'bʌdʒɪt]	preisgünstig einkaufen, im Rahmen des Budgets bleiben
curiosity	[ˌkjʊəri'ɒsəti]	Neugier
to **recommend**	[ˌrekə'mend]	empfehlen
to **pop inside**	['pɒp ˌɪn'saɪd]	schnell hereingehen und nur eine kurze Zeit bleiben
Who cares?	[huː keəz]	Ist doch egal.
features	['fiːtʃəz]	Eigenschaften
wool	[wʊl]	Wolle
synthetic fibres (= man-made fibres)	[sɪn'θetɪk 'faɪbəz]; [ˌmæn'meɪd 'faɪbəz]	Kunstfaser
to **pester**	['pestə]	belästigen
to **buy sth. on a whim**	[baɪ ˌsʌmθɪŋ ɒn ə 'wɪm]	Einen Impulskauf machen
advertising	['ædvətaɪzɪŋ]	Werbung
influence	['ɪnfluəns]	Einfluss
bargain	['bɑːgɪn]	Schnäppchen
discount	['dɪskaʊnt]	Rabatt, Skonto
special offer	['speʃəl 'ɒfə]	Sonderangebot
to **get a deal**	[get ə diːl]	ein Geschäft machen
status-conscious	['steɪtəsˌkɒnʃəs]	standesbewusst
to **admire**	[əd'maɪə]	bewundern
exclusive	[ɪk'skluːsɪv]	exklusiv
organic food	[ɔː'gænɪk fuːd]	Bio-Lebensmittel
to **avoid**	[ə'vɔɪd]	vermeiden
environment	[ɪn'vaɪərənmənt]	Umwelt

chatterbox	['tʃætəbɒks]	Plappermaul, Plaudertasche, Quasselstrippe
to **dither**	['dɪðə]	sich nicht entscheiden können, schwanken, zögern
magpie	['mægpaɪ]	Elster
guarantee	[ˌgærən'tiː]	Garantie, Gewähr
to **suggest**	[sə'dʒest]	vorschlagen
Have you got anything in mind?	[hæv ju gɒt 'eniθɪŋ ɪn maɪnd]	Denken Sie an etwas besonderes?
in two minds	[ɪn tuː maɪndz]	unentschieden
Mind your own business!	[maɪnd jər əʊn 'bɪznəs]	Kümmern Sie sich um Ihre eigenen Sachen!
to **bear in mind**	[beər ɪn maɪnd]	beachten, berücksichtigen
to **change one's mind**	[tʃeɪndʒ wʌnz maɪnd]	sich anders überlegen
in stock	[ɪn stɒk]	vorrätig, am Lager
not in stock (= out of stock)	[nɒt ɪn stɒk]; [aʊt əv stɒk]	nicht vorrätig, nicht lieferbar, vergriffen
demand	[dɪ'mɑːnd]	Nachfrage
to **order**	['ɔːdə]	bestellen
to **take** (time)	[teɪk] ([taɪm])	dauern
by (Friday, Saturday, etc.)	[baɪ] (['fraɪdeɪ/'sætədeɪ])	bis (Freitag, Samstag, usw.)
to **pick** sth./so. **up**	[pɪk ˌsʌmθɪŋ/ˌsʌmwʌn 'ʌp]	etwas abholen
area code	['eəriə ˌkəʊd]	Ortswahl
on (special) **offer**	[ɒn ('speʃəl) 'ɒfə]	im Angebot
floral display	['flɔːrəl dɪ'spleɪ]	Gesteck, Blumenschmuck
lobby	[lɒbi]	Empfangsraum
success	[sək'ses]	Erfolg
to **supply** (with)	[sə'plaɪ (wɪð)]	beliefern, versorgen, bereitstellen, liefern
bouquet	[bʊ'keɪ]	Blumenstrauß
to **launch**	[lɔːntʃ]	einführen, auf den Markt bringen
to **be used** to **sth.**	[bi 'juːzd tʊ ˌsʌmθɪŋ]	an etwas gewöhnt sein
display	[dɪ'spleɪ]	Ausstellung, Schaufensterauslage
to **confirm**	[kən'fɜːm]	bestätigen
If you bear with me a moment.	[ɪf ju beə wɪð mi ə 'məʊmənt]	Wenn Sie ein Moment warten können.

fussy	['fʌsi]	pingelig, kleinlich, penibel, (zu) wählerisch
to **call up**	[ˌkɔːl 'ʌp]	aufrufen
as requested	[æz rɪ'kwestɪd]	wie gewünscht
to **make a note of sth.**	[meɪk ə nəʊt əv ˌsʌmθɪŋ]	etwas vormerken
business card	['bɪznəs ˌkɑːd]	Visitenkarte
to **fill in** (AE: fill out)	[ˌfɪl 'ɪn]; [ˌfɪl 'aʊt]	ausfüllen
form	[fɔːm]	Formular
to **wrap**	[ræp]	verpacken, einwickeln, umhüllen
packaging	['pækɪdʒɪŋ]	Verpackung
carrier bag	['kæriə ˌbæg]	Tragtasche, 'Tüte'
to **gift-wrap**	['gɪftræp]	als Geschenk einpacken
present	['prezənt]	Geschenk
to **squeeze**	[skwiːz]	drücken, pressen, ausquetschen
power drill	['paʊə ˌdrɪl]	Bohrmaschine
out of order	[ˌaʊt əv 'ɔːdə]	außer Betrieb
hard drive	'hɑːd ˌdraɪv	Festplatte
chain	[tʃeɪn]	Kette
to **reply** (to)	[rɪ'plaɪ (tu)]	antworten, beantworten
With best regards	[wɪð best rɪ'gɑːdz]	Mit freundlichen Grüßen
option	['ɒpʃən]	(Wahl)Möglichkeit
unfortunately	[ˌʌn'fɔːtʃənətli]	leider
decision	[dɪ'sɪʒən]	Entscheidung
rap	[ræp]	klopfen, Rap (rhythmischer Sprechgesang), quatschen
wrap	[ræp]	einführen, auf den Markt bringen
scent	[sent]	Duft
warehouse	['weəhaʊs]	Lager, Lagerhalle, Depot
jewellery (AE: **jewelry**)	['dʒuːəlri]	Schmuck
locked cabinet	[ˌlɒkt 'kæbɪnət]	verschlossener Schrank
for security reasons	[fɔː sɪ'kjʊərəti ˌriːzənz]	aus Sicherheitsgründen
to **taste**	[teɪst]	(hier) probieren
wine-tasting	['waɪnˌteɪstɪŋ]	Weinprobe
experts	['ekspɜːts]	Fachleute, 'Kenner'
insurance	[ɪn'ʃʊərəns]	Versicherung

fragile	['frædʒaɪl]	zerbrechlich
to **depend** (on)	[dɪ'pend (ɒn)]	abhängen (auf)
to **invent**	[ɪn'vent]	erfinden
to **appear**	[ə'pɪə]	erscheinen, vorkommen
perishable	['perɪʃəbl]	(leicht) verderblich
security	[sɪ'kjʊərəti]	Sicherheit (gegen Kriminalität od. Verlust)
safety	['seɪfti]	Sicherheit (gegen Gefahr od. körperl. Verletzung)

Unit 4 – Money matters

to **count**	[kaʊnt]	zählen
to **add up**	[ˌæd 'ʌp]	zusammenzählen, addieren, berechnen
total	['təʊtəl]	Gesamtbetrag
amount	[ə'maʊnt]	Betrag, Menge
result	[rɪ'zʌlt]	Ergebnis
bread roll (AE: **bun**)	['bred ˌrəʊl]; [bʌn]	Brötchen
washing-up liquid	[ˌwɒʃɪŋ'ʌp ˌlɪkwɪd]	Spülmittel
whipping cream	['wɪpɪŋ ˌkriːm]	Schlagsahne
in slices	[ɪn 'slaɪsɪz]	in Scheiben geschnitten
olive oil	['ɒlɪv ˌɔɪl]	Olivenöl
raspberry jam	['rɑːzbəri ˌdʒæm]	Himbeermarmelade
tin (AE: **can**)	[tɪn]; [kæn]	Dose
jam (AE: **jelly**)	[dʒæm]; ['dʒeli]	Marmelade
value added tax (VAT) (AE: sales tax)	[ˌvæljuːˌædɪd 'tæks]; [ˌviː eɪ 'tiː]; ['seɪlz ˌtæks]	Umsatzsteuer, Mehrwertsteuer
height	[haɪt]	Größe, Höhe
% off	[pə'sent ɒf]	% billiger
to **save**	[seɪv]	sparen
to **resist**	[rɪ'zɪst]	widerstehen
to **put the prices up**	[pʊt ðə 'praɪsɪz ʌp]	die Preise erhöhen
briefcase	['briːfkeɪs]	Aktentasche, Mappe
skinflint	['skɪnflɪnt]	Geizhals
to **run out of** sth.	[ˌrʌn 'aʊt əv ˌsʌmθɪŋ]	nicht mehr von etwas haben
suitcase	['sjuːtkeɪs]	Koffer
reduction	[rɪ'dʌkʃən]	Preisnachlass

cash discount	['kæʃ ˌdɪskaʊnt]	Skonto
to **come down on the price**	[kʌm daʊn ɒn ðə praɪs]	den Preis (etwas) reduzieren
to **drop prices**	[drɒp 'praɪsiz]	Preise senken
to **afford**	[ə'fɔːd]	sich leisten
installation	[ˌɪnstə'leɪʃən]	Installation, Inbetriebnahme
to **pay in one lump**	[peɪ ɪn wʌn lʌmp]	einen Pauschalpreis zahlen
reasonable	['riːzənəbl]	(hier) akzeptabel
to **pay in instalments**	[peɪ ɪn ɪn'stɔːlmənts]	in Raten zahlen
printer	['prɪntə]	Drucker
cookery book	['kʊkəri ˌbʊk]	Kochbuch
invoice	['ɪnvɔɪs]	Rechnung
net	[net]	Netto
gross	[grəʊs]	Brutto
quantity	['kwɒntəti]	Menge, Quantität
unit price	['juːnɪt ˌpraɪs]	Einzelpreis, Stückpreis
total amount	[ˌtəʊtəl ə'maʊnt]	Gesamtbetrag, Gesamtpreis
order date	['ɔːdə ˌdeɪt]	Bestelldatum
payable within	['peɪəbl wɪ'ðɪn]	zahlbar innerhalb
number of items	['nʌmbər əv 'aɪtəmz]	Menge
order	['ɔːdə]	Bestellung, Auftrag
description of articles	[dɪ'skrɪpʃən əv 'ɑːtɪklz]	Artikelbechreibung
size	[saɪz]	Größe
delivery charge	[dɪ'lɪvəri tʃɑːdʒ]	Versandkosten, Versandgebühr
currently valid	['kʌrəntli 'vælɪd]	derzeit gültig
to **issue**	['ɪʃuː]	ausstellen
skirt	[skɜːt]	Rock
towel	['taʊəl]	Badetuch
to **fetch**	[fetʃ]	holen
purchase	['pɜːtʃəs]	Einkauf
in a hurry	[ɪn ə 'hʌri]	in Eile
to **lend** (to)	[lend (tu)]	leihen, ausleihen (an)
to **borrow** (from)	['bɒrəʊ (frɒm)]	ausleihen (von), borgen
cash	[kæʃ]	bar, Bargeld
debit card	['debɪt ˌkɑːd]	Kundenkarte, EC-Karte
bank transfer	['bæŋk ˌtrænsfɜː]	Banküberweisung

direct debit	['daɪrekt 'debɪt]	per Lastschrift oder Einzügsermächtigung
by cheque (AE: **check**)	[baɪ tʃek]	mit Scheck
to **sign**	['saɪn]	unterschreiben
to **check**	[tʃek]	kontrollieren
successful	[sək'sesfʊl]	erfolgreich
satisfied	['sætɪsfaɪd]	zufrieden
contract	['kɒntrækt]	Vertrag
outstanding (amount, payment)	[ˌaʊt'stændɪŋ]; [ə'maʊnt]; ['peɪmənt]	Restzahlung
down-payment (= deposit)	['daʊnˌpeɪmənt]; [dɪ'pɒzɪt]	Anzahlung
enclosed	[ɪn'kləʊzd]; [ɪŋ-]	in der Anlage, anbei, beigefügt
delay	[dɪ'leɪ]	Verzug, Verspätung
competition	[ˌkɒmpə'tɪʃən]	Preisausschreiben
to **donate**	[dəʊ'neɪt]	spenden
generous	['dʒenərəs]	großzügig
shoplifter	['ʃɒpˌlɪftə]	Ladendieb
to **prosecute**	['prɒsɪkjuːt]	anzeigen, strafrechtlich verfolgen
weight	[weɪt]	Gewicht
due to	[djuː tu]	wegen
counterfeit money	['kaʊntəfɪt 'mʌni]	Falschgeld
to **regret**	[rɪ'gret]	bedauern
to **select**	[sɪ'lekt]	wählen
to **deposit** (money)	[dɪ'pɒzɪt]	einzahlen
to **withdraw** (money)	[wɪð'drɔː]	abheben
to **transfer** (money)	[træns'fɜː]	überweisen
to **exchange** (money)	[ɪks'tʃeɪndʒ]	umtauschen
to **steal** (money)	[stiːl]	klauen
debt	[det]	Schuld
solution	[sə'luːʃən]	Lösung
interest-free	['ɪntrəstˌfriː]	zinsfrei
interest	['ɪntrəst]	Zinsen
additional amount	[ə'dɪʃənəl ə'maʊnt]	(hier) Restbetrag
to **owe**	[əʊ]	schulden
head start	['hedˌstɑːt]	Vorsprung
to **waste**	[weɪst]	verschwenden
change	[tʃeɪndʒ]	Kleingeld, Wechselgeld

cash machine	['kæʃ mə,ʃiːn]	Geldautomat
overdrawn	[,əʊvə'drɔːn]	überzogen
reasonable	['riːzənəbl]	vernünftig
to **overcharge**	[,ɔʊvə'tʃɑːdʒ]	zu viel berechnen od. verlangen
to **weigh**	[weɪ]	wiegen

Unit 5 – Advertising and Promotion

myth	[mɪθ]	Mythos, Fabel
legend	['ledʒənd]	Legende
kilt	[kɪlt]	Schottenrock
belt	[belt]	Gürtel
waistcoat	['weɪstkəʊt]	Weste
pottery	['pɒtəri]	Keramik
copper	['kɒpə]	Kupfer
castle	[kɑːsl]	Schloss, Burg
magic	['mædʒɪk]	Zauber
salmon	['sæmən]	Lachs
fudge	[fʌdʒ]	Fondant, aromatisierte Zuckermasse, Karamel
bagpipe	['bægpaɪp]	Dudelsack
dragon	['drægən]	Drache
raven	['reɪvən]	Rabe
knot	[nɒt]	Knoten
necklace	['nekləs]	Halskette
harp	[hɑːp]	Harfe
bracelet	['breɪslət]	Armband, Armreifen
coin	[kɔɪn]	Münze
plate	[pleɪt]	Teller, Platte, Scheibe
goblet	['gɒblət]	Kelch
cultlery	['kʌtləri]	Besteck
cereal	['sɪəriəl]	Getreide, Getreidepflanze
ingredient	[ɪn'griːdiənt]; [ɪŋ-]	Zutat, Inhaltstoff
to **announce**	[ə'naʊns]	ankündigen
distillery	[dɪ'stɪləri]	Brennerei, Destille
smoked salmon	[sməʊkt 'sæmən]	Räucherlachs
scrambled eggs	[skræmbld egz]	Rührei

oatcake	['əʊtkeɪk]	Haferkeks
breakfast bacon	['brekfəst 'beɪkən]	Frühstücksschinken
lively	['laɪvli]	lebhaft
unique	[ˌjuː'niːk]	einzigartig
fabulous	['fæbjələs]	fabelhaft
to **enter a quiz**	['entərəkwɪz]	an einem Quiz teilnehmen
to **be lucky**	[bi 'lʌki]	Glück haben
high-heeled shoes	[ˌhaɪhiːld 'ʃuːz]	Stöckelschuhe
studded	['stʌdɪd]	verziert, beschlagen
denim	['denɪm]	Jeansstoff
spotted	['spɒtɪd]	mit Pünktchen
snakeskin	['sneɪkskɪn]	Schlangenleder
stonewashed	['stəʊnwɒʃt]	mit Steinen ausgewaschen
hand-crafted, crafted	['hændkrɑːftɪd]	handgemacht, handwerklich hergestellt
bandana	[bæn'dænə]	Halstuch
buckle	[bʌkl]	Schnalle, Spange
suitable	['sjuːtəbl]	geeignet
vegetarian	[ˌvedʒɪ'teəriən]	Vegetarier/in
prize	[praɪz]	Preis
winner	['wɪnə]	Gewinner/in
lucky dip	['lʌki dɪp]	Glückstopf
voucher	['vaʊtʃə]	Gutschein
sample	['sɑːmpl]	(Kost)Probe
to **taste**	[teɪst]	kosten, probieren, schmecken
raffle	[ræfl]	Tombola
case	[keɪs]	Kiste
key ring	[kiː rɪŋ]	Schlüsselring
cherry tomatoes	['tʃeri tə'mɑːəʊz]	Kirschtomaten
nutty bread sticks	['nʌti bred stɪks]	Knabberstangen mit Nußgeschmack
benefit	['benəfɪt]	Vorteil
vineyard	['vɪnjəd]	Weinberg, Weingarten
promotions	[prə'məʊʃənz]	Werbekampagne, Sonderangebot
employment status	[ɪm'plɔɪmənt 'steɪtəs]	berufliche Angaben
title (= form of address)	[taɪtl]; [fɔːm əv ə'dres]	Anrede (Herr, Frau, Dr. ...)
accommodation	[əˌkɒmə'deɪʃən]	Unterkunft

gross annual income	[grəʊs 'ænjuəl 'ɪnkʌm]	Bruttohaushaltseinkommen (pro Jahr)
postcode	['pəʊstkəʊd]	Postleitzahl
nationality	[ˌnæʃə'næləti]	Staatsbürgerschaft, Nationalität
marital status	['mærɪtəl 'steɪtəs]	Familienstand
single	[sɪŋgl]	ledig
married	['mærid]	verheiratet
banking details	['bæŋkɪŋ 'diːteɪlz]	Bankverbindung
credit limit	['kredɪt 'lɪmɪt]	Verfügungsrahmen (für die Bezahlkarte)
date of birth	[deɪt əv bɜːθ]	Geburtsdatum
landline telephone	['lændlaɪn 'telɪfəʊn]	Festnetz
employer	[ɪm'plɔɪə]	Arbeitgeber
rented flat (AE: rented apartment)	['rentɪd 'flæt]; ['rentɪd ə'pɑːrtmənt]	Mietwohnung
account number	[ə'kaʊnt 'nʌmbə]	Kontonummer
sort code	['sɔːt ˌkəʊd]	Bankleitzahl
divorced	[dɪ'vɔːst]	geschieden
to **earn**	[ɜːn]	verdienen
citizen	['sɪtɪzən]	Staatsbürger
to **download**	[ˌdaʊn'ləʊd]	herunterladen
to **preheat**	[ˌpriː'hiːt]	vorheizen
to **grease**	[griːs]	einfetten
to **line with greaseproof paper**	[laɪn wɪð ˌgriːspruːf 'peɪpə]	mit Backpapier auslegen
to **dust with flour**	[dʌst wɪð 'flaʊə]	mit Mehl bestäuben
to **beat the ingredients**	[biːt ði ɪn'griːdiənts]	die Zutaten verrühren
to **pour the mixture into the tin**	[pɔː ðə 'mɪkstʃər ˌɪntu ðə tɪn]	den Teig in die Kuchenform geben
to **bake**	[beɪk]	backen
to **allow to cool**	[ə'laʊ tu kuːl]	auskühlen lassen
skin care	['skɪn ˌkeə]	Hautpflege
label	['leɪbəl]	Etikett
to **contain**	[kən'teɪn]	enthalten
pomegranate	['pɒmɪˌgrænɪt]	Granatapfel
protection	[prə'tekʃən]	Schutz
sensitive	['sensɪtɪv]	empfindlich

to **apply for a job**	[ə'plaɪ fər ə dʒɒb]	sich für eine Stelle bewerben
curriculum vitae (AE: **résumé**)	[kə'rɪkjələm 'viːtaɪ]; ['rezʊmeɪ]	Lebenslauf
application letter	[ˌæplɪ'keɪʃən 'letə]	Bewerbungsschreiben (Begleitbrief zum Lebenslauf)
enthusiastic	[ɪnˌθjuːzi'æstɪk]	einsatzfreudig
to **check stock**	[ˌtʃek 'stɒk]	Lagerbestand kontrollieren
customer care	['kʌstəmə keə]	Kundenpflege
salary	['sæləri]	Gehalt
negotiable	[nɪ'gəʊʃiəbl]	Verhandlungssache
vacancy	['veɪkənsi]	freie Stelle, Stellenangebot
to **specialise in**	['speʃəlaɪz ɪn]	spezialisieren auf
covering letter	['kʌvərɪŋ 'letə]	Begleitbrief
application	[ˌæplɪ'keɪʃən]	Bewerbung
edition	[ɪ'dɪʃən]	Ausgabe
vocational college	[və'keɪʃənəl 'kɒlɪdʒ]	Berufsschule
exchange pupil	[ɪks'tʃeɪndʒ 'pjuːpəl]	Austauschschüler/in
education	[ˌedʒʊ'keɪʃən]	schulische Ausbildung
training	['treɪnɪŋ]	berufliche Ausbildung
interview	['ɪntəvjuː]	(hier) Vorstellungsgespräch
Yours sincerely	[jɔːz sɪn'sɪəli]	Mit freundlichen Grüßen
heading	['hedɪŋ]	Überschrift
questionnaire	[ˌkwestʃə'neə]	Fragebogen, Umfrage
interior design	[ɪn'tɪəriə dɪ'zaɪn]	Raumgestaltung
event	[ɪ'vent]	Veranstaltung
ashtray	['æʃtreɪ]	Aschenbecher
Pleased to meet you.	[pliːzd tə miːt ju]	Es freut mich, Sie kennen zu lernen.
Cheers!	[tʃɪəz]	Zum Wohl!
celebrities	[sə'lebrətiz]	Prominenz

Unit 6 – Sales talk step-by-step

choice	[tʃɔɪs]	Wahl, Auswahl
improvement	[ɪm'pruːvmənt]	Verbesserung
home improvement	[həʊm ɪm'pruːvmənt]	Heimwerken

workbench	['wɜːkbentʃ]	Arbeitsbank
adjustable	[ə'dʒʌstəbl]	einstellbar
pull-out	['pʊlaʊt]	ausziehbar
keyboard	['kiːbɔːd]	Tastatur
carrying case	['kæriɪŋ ˌkeɪs]	(hier) Koffer
to **comprise**	[kəm'praɪz]	beinhalten, bestehen aus, umfassen
stained	[steɪnd]	(hier) gebeizt
treated	['triːtɪd]	behandelt
fixtures and fittings	['fɪkstʃəz ən 'fɪtɪŋz]	bewegliche und unbewegliche Einrichtungsgegenstände
assembly	[ə'sembli]	Montage
craftsmanship	['krɑːftsmənʃɪp]	Handwerkskunst
to **contribute (to)**	[kən'trɪbjuːt tu]	beitragen
incredibly	[ɪn'kredɪbli]; [ɪŋ-]	unglaublich
to **breathe**	[briːð]	atmen
to **last**	[lɑːst]	halten, dauern
to **discover**	[dɪ'skʌvə]	entdecken
sky blue	[skaɪ bluː]	himmelblau
burgundy red	['bɜːgəndi red]	weinrot
fabulous	['fæbjələs]	fabelhaft
eye-catching	['aɪˌkætʃɪŋ]	auffällig, ins Auge springend, auffallend
unusual	[ʌn'juːʒəl]	ungewöhnlich
frost-proof	['frɒstpruːf]	frostsicher
smooth	[smuːð]	glatt, eben
linseed oil	['lɪnsiːd ˌɔɪl]	Leinöl
carpet	['kɑːpɪt]	Teppich
rug	[rʌg]	Vorleger, kleiner, dicker Teppich
hardwearing	[ˌhɑːd'weərɪŋ]	strapazierfähig
to **go well with sth.**	[gəʊ wel wɪð ˌsʌmθɪŋ]	passen gut mit etw.
weave	[wiːv]	Gewebe
hand-woven	[ˌhænd'wəʊvən]	handgewebt
to **greet**	[griːt]	begrüßen
to **maintain**	[meɪn'teɪn]	erhalten, aufrechterhalten, führen

to **state a price**	[ˌsteɪtə'praɪs]	einen Preis angeben od. nennen
confident	['kɒnfɪdənt]	zuversichtlich
'Feel free ...'	[fiːl friː]	'Machen Sie ruhig'
dried	[draɪd]	getrocknet
aerosol spray	['eərəsɒl spreɪ]	Sprühdose
unwrapped	[ʌn'ræpt]	ausgepackt, ungepackt, entpackt
knife (pl. **knives**)	[naɪf]; [naɪvz]	Messer
power tool	['paʊə tuːl]	Elektrowerkzeug
to **restore**	[rɪ'stɔː]	restaurieren
to **drill**	[drɪl]	bohren
concrete	['kɒŋkriːt]	Beton
to **include**	[ɪn'kluːd]; [ɪŋ-]	beinhalten
charger	['tʃɑːdʒə]	(Batterie)Ladegerät
to **charge**	[tʃɑːdʒ]	(hier) laden
tablecloth	['teɪblklɒθ]	Tischdecke
gorgeous	['gɔːdʒəs]	wunderschön
rectangular	[rek'tæŋgjələ]	rechteckig
dining room	['daɪnɪŋ ˌrʊm]	Esszimmer
huge	[hjuːdʒ]	riesig
bright	[braɪt]	bunt, hell
garish	['geərɪʃ]	grell
tasteful	['teɪstfʊl]	geschmackvoll
olive leaf	['ɒlɪv ˌliːf]	Olivenblatt
butterfly	['bʌtəflaɪ]	Schmetterling
napkin (AE: **serviette**)	['næpkɪn]; [ˌsɜːrvi'et]	Serviette
to **match (with)**	[mætʃ (wɪð)]	anpassen an, zusammen-passen
price-conscious	['praɪsˌkɒnʃəs]	preisbewusst
brand-conscious	['brændˌkɒnʃəs]	markenbewusst
to **prevent**	[prɪ'vent]	bohren
windproof	['wɪndpruːf]	windfest
to **look**	[lʊk]	(hier) aussehen
to **taste**	[teɪst]	schmecken
to **feel**	[fiːl]	(hier) sich fühlen
to **sound**	[saʊnd]	klingen
to **smell**	[smel]	riechen
slim	[slɪm]	schlank

tinny	['tɪni]	blechern
powerful	['paʊəfəl]	kräftig
goggles	[gɒglz]	Schutzbrille
stretch fabric	[stretʃ 'fæbrɪk]	dehnbarer Stoff
sales pitch	[seɪlz pɪtʃ]	Verkaufsargument
to **enable**	[ɪn'eɪbl]	ermöglichen
objection	[əb'dʒekʃən]	Einwand
steam	[stiːm]	Dampf
wobbly	['wɒbli]	wacklig, wabbelig
limescale	['laɪmskeɪl]	Kalkablagerung
edges	['edʒɪz]	Kanten
to **fit into**	[fɪt 'ɪntu]	hineinpassen
fuzzy	['fʌzi]	(hier) unscharf
scratched	[skrætʃt]	zerkratzt
to **assure**	[ə'ʃʊə]	zusichern, versprechen
to **adjust**	[ə'dʒʌst]	anpassen, einstellen, justieren, korrigieren
water-softener	['wɔːtəˌsɒfənə]	Wasserenthärtungsgerät
cushion	['kʊʃən]	Kissen
to **prevent**	[prɪ'vent]	verhindern
vacuum cleaner	['vækjuːm ˌkliːnə]	Staubsauger
barbecue set	['bɑːbɪkjuː set]	Grill (mit Zubehör)
sunglasses (AE: **shades**)	['sʌnˌglɑːsɪz]; [ʃeɪdz]	Sonnenbrille
lawnmower	['lɔːnˌməʊə]	Rasenmäher
maintenance	['meɪntənəns]	Wartung, Instandhaltung
garden gnome	['gɑːdən nəʊm]	Gartenzwerg
to **pay in instalments**	[peɪ ɪn ɪn'stɔːlmənts]	in Raten zahlen
loan	[ləʊn]	Kredit, Darlehen
accessible	[ək'sesəbl]	zugänglich, leicht erreichbar

Unit 7 – On the spot

scarf	[skɑːf]	Schal, Halstuch
handy	['hændi]	praktisch
rip-off	['rɪpɒf]	Nepp, Absockerei
to **cost a fortune**	[ˌkɒstə'fɔːtʃːun]	ein Vermögen kosten
frying pan	['fraɪɪŋ ˌpæn]	Bratpfanne

pricey	['praɪsi]	teuer
chainsaw	['tʃeɪnsɔː]	Kettensäge
firewood	['faɪəwʊd]	Brennholz
cutting bar	['kʌtɪŋ bɑː]	Klinge, Blatt
to **tackle**	[tækl]	bewältigen, schaffen, fertig werden mit
lens	[lens]	Linse
impressive	[ɪm'presɪv]	beeindrückend
heel	[hiːl]	Absatz
wedding	['wedɪŋ]	Hochzeit
to **estimate**	['estɪmeɪt]	schätzen
engagement ring	[ɪn'geɪdʒmənt ˌrɪŋ]	Verlobungsring
groom	[gruːm]	Bräutigam
bridal outfit	['braɪdəl 'aʊtfɪt]	Brautkleid und Brautschleier
lingerie	['lǣndʒəri]	Damenunterwäsche
reception	[rɪ'sepʃən]	(hier) Hochzeitsempfang
honeymoon	['hʌnimuːn]	Flitterwoche
unfortunately	[ʌn'fɔːtʃənətli]	leider
trolley (AE: shopping cart)	['trɒli]; ['ʃɒpɪŋ kaːrt]	Einkaufswagen
to **accompany**	[ə'kʌmpəni]	begleiten
chocolate bar	['tʃɒklət ˌbɑː]	Schokoriegel
identity card	[aɪ'dentəti ˌkɑːd]	Ausweis
evidence	['evɪdəns]	Beweis, Nachweis
proof	[pruːf]	Beweis
to **consume**	[kən'sjuːm]	(hier) verzehren
on behalf of	[ɒn bɪ'hɑːf əv]	für, im Auftrag von
value	['væljuː]	Wert
to **return sth.**	[rɪ'tɜːn ˌsʌmθɪŋ]	etwas zurückbringen
polite	[pə'laɪt]	höflich
shoplifting	['ʃɒplɪftɪŋ]	Ladendiebstahl
fur coat	['fɜː ˌkəʊt]	Pelzmantel
to **set off an alarm**	[set ɒf ən ə'lɑːm]	einen Alarm auslösen
to **apologise**	[ə'pɒlədʒaɪz]	sich entschuldigen, um Verzeihung bitten
apology	[ə'pɒlədʒi]	Entschuldigung
incident	['ɪnsɪdənt]	Vorfall, Ereignis
to **occur**	[ə'kɜː]	passieren, geschehen
humiliating	[hjuː'mɪlieɪtɪŋ]	demütigend

to **apprehend**	[ˌæprɪ'hend]	fassen, festnehmen
to **enquire**	[ɪn'kwaɪə]; [ɪŋ-]	anfragen
employee	[ɪm'plɔɪiː]	Arbeitnehmer
duty	['djuːti]	Pflicht
to **search**	[sɜːtʃ]	untersuchen, durchsuchen
to **suspect**	[sə'spekt]	verdächtigen
to **insist on**	[ɪn'sɪst ɒn]	bestehen auf
to **inspect**	[ɪn'spekt]	untersuchen, prüfen
to **make a complaint**	[ˌmeɪkəkəm'pleɪnt]	eine Beschwerde od. Reklamation machen
to **accuse**	[ə'kjuːz]	beschuldigen
senior citizen	[ˌsiːniə 'sɪtɪzən]	Rentner, Pensionär
criminal	['krɪmɪnəl]	Verbrecher
upset	[ʌp'set]	aufgeregt
confidence	['kɒnfɪdəns]	Vertrauen
to **appreciate**	[ə'priːʃieɪt]	(hier) dankbar sein, begrüßen
embarrassing	[ɪm'bærəsɪŋ]	peinlich
to **consider**	[kən'sɪdə]	überlegen, in Erwägung ziehen
satisfactory	[ˌsætɪs'fæktəri]	zufriedenstellend
lawyer	['lɔːjə]	Rechtsanwalt
progress	['prəʊgres]	Fortschritt

Unit 8 – After-sales

to **recognise**	['rekəgnaɪz]	(wieder)erkennen
mess	[mes]	Unordnung, Dreck
generous	['dʒenərəs]	großzügig
food processor	['fuːd ˌprəʊsesə]	Küchenmaschine
water pressure	['wɔːtə ˌpreʃə]	Wasserdruck
instruction manual	[ɪn'strʌkʃən ˌmænjuəl]	Handbuch
engineer	[ˌendʒɪ'nɪə]	(hier) Techniker
fault	[fɔːlt]	(hier) Schuld
annoying	[ə'nɔɪɪŋ]	ärgerlich
to **bother**	['bɒðə]	sich die Mühe machen
damaged	['dæmɪdʒd]	beschädigt
flawed	[flɔːd]	fehlerhaft

incomplete	[ˌɪnkəm'pliːt]	unvollständig
missing	['mɪsɪŋ]	fehlend
substandard	[sʌb'stændəd]	minderwertig
delayed	[dɪ'leɪd]	verspätet
lost in transit	[lɒst ɪn 'trænzɪt]	auf dem Transportweg verlorengegangen
to **break down**	[breɪk daʊn]	versagen, eine Panne haben, zusammenbrechen
to **grant a discount**	[ˌgrɑːntə'dɪskaʊnt]	einen Preisnachlass geben od. gewähren
refund	[rɪ'fʌnd]	Rückerstattung
to **replace**	[rɪ'pleɪs]	ersetzen
substitute	['sʌbstɪtjuːt]	Ersatz
credit note	['kredɪt ˌnəʊt]	Gutschrift
compensation	[ˌkɒmpən'seɪʃən]	Entschädigung
to **admit**	[əd'mɪt]	zugeben, gestehen
to **empathise**	['empəθaɪz]	Mitleid od. Mitgefühl zeigen
silk blouse	[sɪlk blaʊz]	Seidenbluse
flaw	[flɔː]	Fehler, Makel, Sprung, Riss, Fehlerstelle
to **exchange**	[ɪks'tʃeɪndʒ]	umtauschen, austauschen
on vacation, (BE: **on holiday**)	[ɒn veɪ'keɪʃən]; [ɒn 'hɒlədeɪ]	im Urlaub
screwdriver	['skruːˌdraɪvə]	Schraubenzieher
to **lock**	[lɒk]	zuschließen
trouble	[trʌbl]	Ärger
inconvenience	[ˌɪnkən'viːniəns]	Unannehmlichkeiten
impregnation	[ˌɪmpreg'neɪʃən]	Imprägnierung
to **make up for sth.**	[meɪk ʌp fə ˌsʌmθɪŋ]	wiedergutmachen, ausgleichen, wettmachen
suggestion	[sə'dʒestʃən]	Vorschlag
counter	['kaʊntə]	Theke
hygiene	['haɪdʒiːn]	Hygiene
to **remind**	[rɪ'maɪnd]	erinnern
cart (BE: **shopping trolley**)	[kɑːrt]; ['ʃɒpɪŋ ˌtrɒli]	Einkaufswagen
thief (pl. **thieves**)	[θiːf]; [θiːvz]	Dieb
bin liner	['bɪn ˌlaɪnə]	Müllsack
groceries	['grəʊsəriz]	Lebensmittel

sign	[saɪn]	Schild
arrow	['ærəʊ]	Pfeil
restroom, (BE: **toilet**)	['restruːm]; ['tɔɪlət]	Toilette
night shift	['naɪt ˌʃɪft]	Nachtschicht
disabled	[dɪ'səɪbld]	behindert
delivery service	[dɪ'lɪvəri 'sɜːvɪs]	Lieferservice
aisle	[aɪl]	Gang
narrow	['nærəʊ]	eng
to **get stuck**	[get stʌk]	stecken bleiben
to **protect**	[prə'tekt]	schützen
to **dry-clean**	[ˌdraɪ'kliːn]	reinigen
dissatisfied	[dɪs'sætɪsfaɪd]	unzufrieden
bang	[bæŋ]	Knall
broken glass	[ˌbrəʊkən 'glɑːs]	Glasscherben
dangerous	['deɪndʒərəs]	gefährlich
injured	['ɪndʒəd]	verletzt
blinded	['blaɪndɪd]	geblendet
electricity	[ˌelɪk'trɪsəti]	Strom
zip (AE: **zipper**)	[zɪp]; ['zɪpər]	Reisverschluss
immediately	[ɪ'miːdiətli]	sofort
solution	[sə'luːʃən]	Lösung
agreed	[ə'griːd]	vereinbart
to **escape**	[ɪ'skeɪp]	entkommen
injury	['ɪndʒəri]	Verletzung
to **cause**	[kɔːz]	verursachen
distress	[dɪ'stres]	Leiden, Kummer, Sorge
to **value**	['væljuː]	(hier) schätzen
concerned	[kən'sɜːnd]	besorgt
alarming	[ə'lɑːmɪŋ]	besorgniserregend
voucher	['vaʊtʃə]	Gutschein
recall	[rɪ'cɔːl]	Rückrufaktion
strict	[strɪkt]	streng
to **fail**	[feɪl]	versagen
for safety reasons	[fə 'seɪfti ˌriːzənz]	aus Sicherheitsgründen
to **burst**	[bɜːst]	platzen
accident	['æksɪdənt]	Unfall
to **avoid**	[ə'vɔɪd]	vermeiden
to **swallow**	['swɒləʊ]	schlucken

to **inhale**	[ɪn'heɪl]	einatmen
to **affect**	[ə'fekt]	betreffen, beinträchtigen
to **kindly ask**	[ˌkaɪndli 'ɑːsk]	höflich bitten
to **make sure**	[ˌmeɪk' ʃɔː]	sicherstellen, versichern
out of reach	[aʊt əv riːtʃ]	aus der Reichweite
to **regret**	[rɪ'gret]	bedauern
measure	['meʒə]	Maßnahme
to **review**	[rɪ'vjuː]	(hier) prüfen
concerned	[kən'sɜːnd]	besorgt
chipped	[tʃɪpt]	abgeplatzt, abgeraspelt, abgeschnitzelt
faded	['feɪdɪd]	abgefärbt, verblasst
discoloured	[dɪ'skʌləd]	verfärbt
twisted	['twɪstɪd]	krumm, verdreht, sich verknackst
torn	[tɔːn]	zerissen, gerissen, durchgerissen
bent	[bent]	gebeugt, verbogen, krumm
stained	[steɪnd]	befleckt, beschmutzt, fleckig
leaking	['liːkɪŋ]	tropfend, undicht seinend, auslaufend
dented	['dentɪd]	eingebeult, verbeult, eingedellt, eingedrückt
mail order house	[ˌmeɪlɔːdə 'haʊs]	Versandhaus

Alphabetical word list

AE: American English (AmE)
BE: British English (BrE)

ENGLISH	EXAMPLES AND USAGE	GERMAN
accessory	Belts and scarves are accessories.	*Zubehör*
accommodation	House and flats are types of accommodation.	*Unterkunft*
account number	Our account number and bank sort code are on the invoice.	*Kontonummer*
to accuse	I was wrongly accused of shoplifting.	*anschuldigen; beschuldigen*
to adjust	You can adjust the brightness by pressing this button.	*verstellen; anpassen*
adjustable	an adjustable spanner	*verstellbar*
to advertise	to advertise a product / to advertise for an assistant	*werben für*
advertisement	Short forms: an advert / an ad	*Werbung; Reklame*
advertising	an advertising campaign	*Werbung (als Tätigkeit)*
afford	I can't afford anything more expensive.	*sich etwas leisten*
after-sales	the service to the customer after the sale	*Kundendienst*
aisle	'Aisle' rhymes with 'I'll' and 'isle'	*Gang (im Supermarkt oder Flugzeug)*
amount	If you buy a large amount, you might get a discount.	*Betrag; Menge*
to apologise	I would like to apologise for the mistake.	*sich entschuldigen*
apology	Please accept my apologies.	*Entschuldigung*
appliance	A toaster is a kitchen appliance.	*Elektrogerät*
application	a job application an application for a bank loan	*Bewerbung; Antrag*
application form	Have you filled in the application form yet?	*Antragsformular*
to apply for	Are you going to apply for the job? Lots of customers have applied for our store card.	*bewerben; beantragen*
apprentice	an apprentice carpenter	*Auszubildende / r (in einem Gewerbe)*

ENGLISH	EXAMPLES AND USAGE	GERMAN
apprenticeship	to do an apprenticeship	*Ausbildung; eine Ausbildung machen*
to arrest	He was arrested for shoplifting.	*verhaften*
to assemble	You need to assemble the table yourself.	*zusammenbauen*
assembly	The assembly is easy.	*Zusammenbau*
to assure	I assure you that it won't happen again.	*versprechen; zusichern*
attachment	I can't open the attachment.	*Anhang (E-Mail)*
available	These coffee tables are available in different sizes. We haven't got any blue ones available at the moment.	*erhältlich; verfügbar*
average	I spend an average of €100 (or: €100 on average) a week on groceries.	*Durchschnitt;* *im Durchschnitt*
to avoid	Shop early if you want to avoid queuing.	*vermeiden*
balance	I need to check my bank balance.	*Kontostand*
bargain	I can't resist a bargain.	*Schnäppchen*
benefit	What are the benefits of this storecard?	*Vorteil*
to benefit	How will this product benefit me?	*von Vorteil sein*
bent	The saucepan handle is bent and the lid is dented.	*verbogen*
bestseller	This is our bestseller / our best-selling product.	*Renner*
bill	a $10 bill (BE: note) Save all your bills. They billed me for €456.23.	*Geldschein; Beleg; Rechnung; in Rechnung stellen*
branch	I work in the Grünwald branch of Lidl.	*Filiale*
brand	Which brand of detergent do you prefer?	*Marke*
to browse		*(ziellos) um sich schauen*
to call up	I'll call up the product on my database	*aufrufen*
carrier bag	Some shops charge customers for carrier bags.	*Einkaufstüte*

Vocabulary

ENGLISH	EXAMPLES AND USAGE	GERMAN
carving	Cuckoo-clocks have wooden carvings.	*Schnitzerei*
cash	I'd like to pay in cash.	*bar; Bargeld*
cash desk	I work at / on the cash desk.	*Kasse*
change	Have you got any (small) change?	*Wechselgeld; Kleingeld*
changing room	In the past, these were called 'fitting rooms'.	*Umkleidekabine*
charge	to pay a delivery charge	*Gebühr*
to charge	Do you charge for delivery?	*berechnen; in Rechnung stellen*
	I need to re-charge my battery.	*aufladen*
chatterbox	She talks non-stop. She's a real chat-terbox.	*Quasselstrippe*
checkout	I work at / on the checkout.	*Kasse*
cheque	Can I pay by cheque? (AE check)	*Scheck*
client	Clients are people who pay for a serv-ice.	*Kunde / in; Mandant / in*
coin	a two-euro coin	*Münze*
colleague	AE: co-worker	*Mitarbeiter / in; Kollege / in*
to come down on	Could you come down on the price?	*etwas mit dem Preis machen*
to come with	Does this come with batteries?	*mit etwas ausgestattet sein*
comfortable	a soft and comfortable chair	*bequem; angenehm (physisches Gefühl)*
to compete	to compete with	*konkurrieren mit*
competition	to lose out to / beat the competition to win / lose / take part in a compe-tition	*Konkurrenz; Wettbe-werb; Preisausschreiben*
competitive	a competitive product / price / person	*wettbewerbsfähig; konkurrenzfähig*
competitor	Who is Coca Cola's main competitor? Pepsi!	*Konkurrenz; Konkur-rent*
to complain	to complain about a faulty product	*reklamieren; sich be-schweren*
complaint	to make / lodge a complaint about something	*Reklamation; Beschwerde*
to comprise	The set comprises a table and two chairs.	*aus etwas bestehen; beinhalten*
confidence	I have no confidence in the product.	*Vertrauen*

Vocabulary

ENGLISH	EXAMPLES AND USAGE	GERMAN
conscious	Some customers are very brand-conscious.	*bewusst*
to consist of	The work station consists of three sections.	*aus etwas bestehen; beinhalten*
to contain	This skin cream does not contain gelatine.	*beinhalten*
convenience	I like the convenience of home shopping.	*Bequemlichkeit*
convenient	convenient shopping hours	*bequem (im Sinne von praktisch oder passend)*
cordless	a cordless power drill	*schnurlos*
cosmetics	Lipstick and mascara are examples of cosmetics (or make up).	*Kosmetik*
to count	Please count your change.	*zählen*
counterfeit money	a counterfeit €50 note	*Falschgeld*
covering letter	Send a covering (or: cover) letter with your CV.	*Begleitbrief*
co-worker (AE)	BE: colleague	*Mitarbeiter/in; Kollege/in*
craftsmanship	Carpenters and potters are examples of craftsmen.	*Handwerk*
credit card	Are you paying in cash or by credit card?	*Kreditkarte*
credit limit	The maximum credit limit allowed is €1000.	*Verfügungsrahmen*
credit note	If you return the faulty product, we will give you a credit note.	*Gutschrift; Gutschein*
crockery	cups, plates, bowls, etc.	*Geschirr; Porzellan*
curiosity	I often buy new brands out of curiosity.	*Neugier*
curriculum vitae (CV)	AE: résumé	*Lebenslauf*
customer	Customers buy products and services.	*Kunde/in*
cutlery	knives, forks, spoons, etc.	*Besteck*
damage	The box will protect the goods from damage.	*Schaden*
to damage	The fire damaged the building.	*schädigen*
damaged	We don't take back damaged goods.	*beschädigt*
deal	a good deal	*Geschäft; Abmachung*

ENGLISH	EXAMPLES AND USAGE	GERMAN
degrees	A good room temperature is 22 degrees.	*Grad*
delayed	I'm sorry I'm late. My train was delayed.	*verspätet*
delicious	very tasty	*lecker*
delighted	You will be delighted with your purchase.	*glücklich*
to deliver	The goods will be delivered by the end of the week at the latest.	*liefern*
delivery	Do you charge for delivery?	*Lieferung; Versand*
delivery date	The delivery date is 6th July.	*Liefertermin*
delivery time	The delivery time will be about two weeks.	*Lieferzeit*
demand	a huge demand for a product	*Nachfrage*
to demand	I demand to speak to the manager.	*verlangen; fordern*
department	You'll find the model trains in the toy department.	*Abteilung*
department head	The head of the department	*Abteilungsleiter*
department store	Harrods is a famous London department store.	*Kaufhaus*
depend on	It depends on the weather.	*davon abhängig sein* (It depends: *Es kommt darauf an.)*
deposit	to pay a deposit on something	*Pfand; Anzahlung; Einzahlung; Einlage*
to deposit	to deposit money	*einzahlen*
device	Devices and gadgets are usually small enough to hold in your hand.	*Gerät*
disabled	She has to look after a disabled relative.	*behindert*
disappointing	a disappointing product / service / offer	*enttäuschend*
discoloured	a toothpaste with whitener for discoloured teeth	*verfärbt*
discount	cash discount (for prompt payment) quantity discount (for buying large amounts)	*Skonto; Rabatt*
dissatisfied	He was dissatisfied with the service.	*unzufrieden*
to dither	People who dither find it hard to make up their mind.	*unentschieden sein*

ENGLISH	EXAMPLES AND USAGE	GERMAN
Do-it-Yourself (DIY)	DIY-store	*(selber machen =) Baumarkt*
to donate	Do you ever donate to charities?	*spenden*
donation	That was a generous donation.	*Spende*
to double-check	Double-check the invoice for mistakes.	*zweifach prüfen*
to drop	They have dropped all their prices.	*reduzieren*
durable	hard-wearing or robust	*langlebig; strapazier-fähig*
duty	I am only doing my duty. Making the coffee isn't one of my duties.	*Pflicht; Aufgabe*
economical	An economical car is cheap to run.	*sparsam; ener-giesparend*
efficient	an efficient engine; an efficient member of staff	*effizient; tüchtig; fleißig*
embarrassing	I dropped a bottle of wine. It was so embarrassing!	*peinlich*
to enhance	These candles will enhance the room.	*aufwerten; hier: atmos-phärisch verbessern*
environmentally friendly	not harmful to the environment	*umweltfreundlich*
exchange	in exchange for: in return for	*Austausch; Umtausch*
to exchange	to exchange currency, to exchange goods	*wechseln; umtauschen, austauschen*
expensive	I can't afford it. It's too expensive.	*teuer*
fabric	Some people prefer natural fabrics, such as silk.	*Stoff*
factory outlet	place where brand or designer goods are sold directly to the customer, without involving middlemen	*Outlet, Fabrikverkauf*
to fade		*verblassen*
fault	a fault in the manufacturing I'm sorry, it was my fault.	*Fehler; Schuld*
faulty	It isn't working because the battery is faulty.	*defekt; fehlerhaft*
features	This product has some innovative features.	*Eigenschaften*
Feel free.	Feel free to try any of our new wines.	*Machen Sie ruhig.*
fibre	I am allergic to some synthetic fibres.	*Fasern, Textilien*

ENGLISH	EXAMPLES AND USAGE	GERMAN
to fit with	The camera can be fitted with different lenses.	*ausstatten mit*
fixtures and fittings	Bathroom fixtures and fittings include taps, shower attachments, soap dispensers, etc.	*bewegliche und unbewegliche Einrichtungsgegenstände*
flaw	There is a flaw in the fabric.	*Makel; Fehler; Defekt*
flyer	or: flier	*Flugblatt*
fortune	I spent a fortune on these new shoes.	*Vermögen*
fragile	easily broken	*zerbrechlich*
fragrance	scent	*Duft*
fussy	I'm not fussy about my food.	*wählerisch*
fuzzy	The picture is fuzzy. It's not sharp enough.	*verschwommen; unscharf*
to gain	to gain weight; to gain experience	*gewinnen*
garish	Some people find garish colours tasteless.	*grell*
genuine	It's genuine fur, not imitation.	*echt*
gift	present	*Geschenk*
to gift-wrap	Would you like me to gift-wrap this for you?	*etwas als Geschenk einpacken*
goggles	Skiers wear goggles to protect their eyes from the sun.	*Schutzbrille*
groceries	a bag full of groceries	*Einkäufe (Lebensmittel)*
gross income	income before deductions for tax and social security	*Bruttohaushaltseinkommen*
guarantee	AmE: warranty	*Garantie*
handy	A mobile phone is handy in emergencies.	*nützlich; praktisch*
healthy	healthy food for health-conscious people	*gesund*
height	'Height' rhymes with 'might', 'weight' rhymes with 'wait'	*Höhe*
hygiene	Good hygiene prevents the spread of diseases.	*Hygiene*
to be in charge of	to be responsible for	*zuständig sein; verantwortlich sein*
to have in mind	to have something (special) in mind to have a (particular) price in mind	*an etwas (Besonderes) denken; eine (Preis-) Vorstellung haben*
in stock	We haven't got the goods in stock.	*vorrätig*

ENGLISH	EXAMPLES AND USAGE	GERMAN
to include	The price is €600, including delivery.	*einschließen*
included	The price is €600, delivery included.	*einschließlich*
inconvenience	I do apologise for the inconvenience we have caused.	*Unannehmlichkeiten*
ingredient	The ingredients of Spätzle are flour, water, eggs and a pinch of salt.	*Zutat*
injury	to cause an injury to someone	*Verletzung*
instalment	You can pay in instalments.	*Rate*
instruction manual		*Handbuch*
instructions for use	written explanation of how to do something	*Gebrauchsanweisung*
interest	You pay interest on a loan. (uncountable) The customer showed a lot of interest.	*Zinsen; Interesse*
interview	a job interview an interview with the press	*Vorstellungsgespräch; Interview*
invoice	I received an invoice for $3352.99	*Rechnung*
to invoice	Are you going to invoice me for the goods?	*in Rechnung stellen*
keen	a keen football fan; to be keen on something	*begeistert sein; scharf auf etwas sein*
kiosk	a little shop	*Kiosk*
to launch	to launch a product on a market	*einführen (auf dem Markt)*
laywer	AE: attorney	*Rechtsanwalt*
leak	a leak in a pipe	*Leck*
legal action	I decided to take legal action against the store.	*gerichtliche Schritte*
lingerie	women's underwear (bras, pants, etc.)	*Damen(unter)wäsche; Dessous*
loan	to take out a loan from a bank	*Darlehen; Kredit*
to be located	Our store is located outside the town centre.	*sich befinden*
to look forward to	I look forward to hearing from you.	*sich auf etwas freuen*
to lose	Don't lose the receipt.	*verlieren*
loss	a remedy against hair loss	*Verlust*
to be lost in transit	The goods were lost in transit.	*auf dem Transportweg verloren gegangen sein*

ENGLISH	EXAMPLES AND USAGE	GERMAN
lump sum	You can pay in a lump sum.	*Pauschalsumme*
maintenance	It's cheap to buy, but the maintenance costs are high.	*Wartung und Instandhaltung*
to make up one's mind	Which one should I buy? I can't make up my mind.	*entscheiden*
manager		*Manager; Abteilungsleiter*
manual	A manual is a small book of instructions for use.	*Handbuch; Bedienungsanleitung*
marital status	Adults can be married, divorced, separated, widowed or living together	*Familienstand*
market leader	Who is the market leader in MP3 players?	*Marktführer*
means of identification	Have you got any means of identification, such as a passport or driving license?	*Ausweispapiere*
member of staff	This toilet is only for members of staff / for staff members.	*Mitarbeiter*
to be missing	Some pieces are missing from the jigsaw.	*fehlen*
nationality	My nationality is British, not English.	*Staatsangehörigkeit*
net	a net profit ↔ a gross profit	*netto*
note	a €10 note (AE: bill) I'll make a note of it. / I'll note it down.	*Geldschein* *Notiz; notieren*
objection	to make an objection	*Einwand*
to be off	It's 20% off.	*reduziert (im Preis)*
offer	I'll make you an offer you can't refuse.	*Angebot*
to offer	Can I offer you an alternative?	*anbieten*
old-fashioned	not modern or trendy	*altmodisch*
on a whim	to buy something on a whim	*spontan*
order	to place an order with a company for a product	*Auftrag; Bestellung*
to order	We haven't got any in stock, but we can order some for you.	*bestellen*
organic	organic fruit, organic vegetables	*biologisch*
origin	the country of origin: where the product was made	*Ursprung; Herkunft*
to originate	Cuckoo-clocks originate from the Black Forest.	*stammen aus*

ENGLISH	EXAMPLES AND USAGE	GERMAN
outfit	matching clothes, e.g. for a party	*Outfit*
outlet	any place from where goods are sold	*Verkaufsstelle*
out-of-date	This furniture is very out-of-date.	*altmodisch*
sell-by date	The butter is past its sell-by date.	*Verfallsdatum*
to overcharge	You have overcharged me by 40 cents.	*zu viel in Rechnung stellen*
overpriced	That's overpriced. I'll ask for a reduction.	*zu hoch im Preis*
to overspend	Do credit cards encourage people to overspend?	*mehr ausgeben als geplant*
to owe	I don't owe you anything. I've already paid you back.	*schulden*
packaging	Well-designed packaging can help to sell a product.	*Verkaufsverpackung*
packing	Bubble wrap is good for packing frag-ile items.	*Verpackung*
to pay for	Have you paid for the goods yet?	*bezahlen*
pay in one go	You can pay in one go = in one lump sum	*Pauschalsumme bezahlen*
to pay	I'd like to pay in cash.	*zahlen; bezahlen*
payable	Cheques should be made payable to Trans Euro Travel Ltd.	*zahlbar*
plug	to put in the plug; to plug something in	*Steckdose*
polite	Are you always polite to your custom-ers?	*höflich*
postage and packing	We charge a small fee for postage and packing.	*Porto, Versandkosten*
to prefer	I prefer to shop alone than with friends.	*vorziehen; etwas lieber machen*
preference	This customer has special preferences.	*Vorliebe*
price	to pay a price	*Preis*
price tag	I can't find the price tag on these jeans.	*Preisschild*
priceless	a priceless antique	*von unschätzbarem Wert;*
pricey	very expensive	*teuer*
to print		*drucken*
prize	to win a prize	*Preis (zu gewinnen)*
to produce	These pens were produced in Taiwan.	*herstellen; produzieren*

ENGLISH	EXAMPLES AND USAGE	GERMAN
product	a product, compare: to produce	*Produkt*
product line	products belonging to one category	*Produktlinie*
product range	products belonging to different cate-gories	*Produktsortiment*
product recall	a recall; to recall a product	*Produktrückruf*
to promise	I promise not to do it again.	*versprechen*
proof	A receipt gives proof of payment.	*Beweis*
to prosecute	Shoplifters will be prosecuted.	*anzeigen*
protection	to give protection against	*Schutz*
to prove	Can you prove that you bought it here?	*beweisen*
purchase	a shopping bag full of purchases	*Einkäufe*
to purchase	Children are not allowed to purchase cigarettes.	*kaufen*
to put some-thing by	Would you like me to put this jacket by for you? You can pay later	*etwas zur Seite legen*
range	We have a wide range of bicycle saddles.	*Sortiment; Palette*
reasonable	a reasonable price = a fair price	*erschwinglich; günstig; vernünftig*
receipt	'Receipt' rhymes with 'seat'	*Quittung; Beleg; Kassenbon*
to recommend	Which do you recommend? The red one or the green one?	*empfehlen*
to reduce	Prices have been reduced by 25%.	*reduzieren*
reduction	We can give you a reduction on the price.	*Preisnachlass*
refund	The customer asked for a refund.	*Rückerstattung*
to refund	We refunded the whole amount.	*rückerstatten*
to regret	We regret that the goods are not in stock.	*bedauern; bereuen*
reliable	dependable (opposite: unreliable)	*zuverlässig*
to remove	Remove the plastic film before use.	*entfernen*
to repair	to mend	*reparieren*
to replace	to replace the old batteries with new ones	*ersetzen*
replacement		*Ersatz*
reputation	to have a reputation for quality	*Ruf*

ENGLISH	EXAMPLES AND USAGE	GERMAN
to be responsible for	I'm responsible for after-sales.	*verantwortlich sein für*
retail outlet **retail chain**	A supermarket is a type of retail outlet.	*Einzelhandelsgeschäft* *Einzelhandelskette*
retailer	Person or company that sells to the public.	*Einzelhändler*
retailing	Sales assistants work in retailing.	*Einzelhandel*
rip-off **to rip off**	I paid a fortune for this perfume, but it's mostly packaging. What a rip-off!	*Nepp; Schwindel* *jemanden über's Ohr hauen*
to run out of	I've run out of money. My pen has run out.	*ablaufen; auslaufen; nichts mehr haben*
sale	to be on sale: to be sold at a reduced price the summer / winter sales I haven't made a sale today.	*Sonderangebot; Schlussverkauf; Verkauf*
sales assistant	shop assistant; sales person	*Verkäufer(in)*
sample	I can show you some samples if you like.	*Probe; Muster*
to sample	Would you like to sample this cream cheese dip?	*probieren, kosten*
satisfaction	Customer satisfaction is very important to us.	*Zufriedenheit*
satisfied	I am sure you will be satisfied with your purchase.	*zufrieden*
to save	to save money to buy something to save a person / animal from something	*sparen; retten*
scent	fragrance	*Duft*
scratch	a scratch on a product (verb: to scratch)	*Kratzer*
security	Most big stores have security cameras.	*Sicherheit (gegen Verbrechen / Risiko)*
to select	You can select any item you want.	*auswählen; wählen*
selection	We have a wide selection on perfumes.	*Auswahl*
self-service	a self-service restaurant	*Selbstbedienung*
sell-by date	The butter is past its sell-by date.	*Verfallsdatum*
sensible	You have made a sensible purchase.	*vernünftig*
sensitive	This cream is suitable for sensitive skin.	*empfindlich*

ENGLISH	EXAMPLES AND USAGE	GERMAN
service	Banking and insurance are examples of services.	*Dienstleistung; Service*
to ship	to send by mail / post (esp. AE)	*versenden*
shop (BE) /	a shoe shop (BE); a shoe store (AE) But: a department store (BE / AE)	*Laden; Geschäft* *store (AE)*
shoplifter	Shoplifters come from all walks of society.	*Ladendieb*
shoplifting	stealing from shops	*Ladendiebstahl*
shopping centre	Shopping centres are usually located on the outskirts of towns (AE = shopping mall).	*Einkaufszentrum (BE)*
to sign	Please sign your name here.	*unterschreiben*
signature	The signature on the receipt should match the one on the credit card.	*Unterschrift*
solution	We have a solution to your problem.	*Lösung*
solve	I hope we can solve the problem.	*lösen*
sophisticated	opposite: primitive	*komplex; raffiniert*
sort code	We need your account number and the sort code.	*Bankleitzahl*
special offer	to be on special offer	*Sonderangebot*
spice	Chili is a very hot spice. (adj.: a spicy sauce)	*Gewürz*
staff member		*Mitarbeiter*
stained	The wood has been stained a darker brown. The dress was stained with coffee.	*gebeizt* *beschmutzt, befleckt*
statement	I need to check my bank statement.	*Kontoauszug*
state-of-the-art	a state-of-the-art computer	*neuester Stand der Technik*
to steal	Make sure that nobody steals your credit card.	*stehlen*
strict	We have a strict no-smoking policy.	*streng*
substitute	Margarine is a substitute for butter.	*Ersatz (als Alternative)*
to suit	That colour really suits you!	*gut stehen*
suitable	to be suitable for (noun. suitability)	*geeignet*
supermarket	a shop which sells all kinds of food and household goods	*Supermarkt*
to supervise	to watch over	*betreuen; überwachen*

ENGLISH	EXAMPLES AND USAGE	GERMAN
supervisor	person in charge of a group of people	*Ausbildungsleiter / in; Vorgesetzte / r; Betreuer / in (am Arbeitsplatz)*
supplier	a supplier of a product / service	*Lieferant*
to supply	to supply a customer with a product / service	*beliefern*
to suspect	She was suspected of shoplifting.	*verdächtigen*
to switch on / off	turn on / off	*aus- / abschalten*
synthetic	synthetic fibres, synthetic rubber	*künstlich*
target	Students are our target customers.	*Ziel*
task	Can you manage your tasks without help?	*Aufgabe*
to taste	It tastes delicious. Would you like to taste this new spicy sauce?	*schmecken* *kosten; probieren*
tasteful	a tastefully decorated room	*geschmackvoll*
tasteless	tasteless food; tasteless furniture	*geschmacklos*
tasting	a wine-tasting	*Probe (Weinprobe)*
tasty	a tasty soup	*schmackhaft; lecker*
tinny	The loudspeakers sound tinny.	*blechern*
tool	A hammer is a tool for driving a nail into wood.	*Werkzeug*
to train	I'm training to be a sales assistant.	*ausbilden (beruflich)*
to be trained	I'm not trained in dealing with children.	*ausgebildet sein*
trainee	I'm a trainee sales assistant.	*Auszubildende / r*
training	I'm doing my training in Munich.	*Berufsbildung*
to transfer	I have transferred the money to your account.	*überweisen*
treated	The wood has been fully treated.	*behandelt*
trolley	a shopping trolley; a baggage trolley (AE: cart)	*(Einkaufs- / Gepäck-) Wagen*
trouble	I'm sorry you've had so much trouble.	*Mühe, Ärger*
user-friendly	easy to use or operate	*benutzerfreundlich*
vacancy	I see that you have a vacancy for a sales assistant. The hotel has no vacancies left.	*Stellenangebot; offene Stelle;* *Zimmer frei*
value added tax	AE: sales tax	*Mehrwertsteuer, Umsatzsteuer*

ENGLISH	EXAMPLES AND USAGE	GERMAN
value for money	Our products offer excellent value for money.	*Preis-Leistungs-Verhältnis*
vending machine	a cigarette vending machine	*Automat*
versatile	A versatile product can be used in many different ways.	*vielseitig; wendig*
voucher	a meal voucher worth €10	*Gutschein*
warranty	BrE: guarantee	*Garantie*
waste	That's a waste of time, money and energy.	*Verschwendung*
to waste	Don't waste your money. Save it!	*verschwenden*
to weigh	It only weighs a few grams.	*wiegen*
weight	to lose weight	*Gewicht*
wholesaler	Wholesalers sell to retailers.	*Großhändler*
to win	I've just won a prize!	*gewinnen*
windproof	a windproof, water-resistant anorak	*windfest*
to withdraw	I need to withdraw some cash from my account.	*abheben*
wobbly	The table legs are wobbly.	*wacklig*
to wrap (up)	Shall I wrap that up for you?	*(als Geschenk) einpacken*
zip	AE: zipper	*Reißverschluss*

Symbols and short forms

Short form	Full form	German
asap	as soon as possible	*so bald wie möglich*
BOGOF	Buy one, get one free.	*einen Artikel kaufen, den zweiten gratis dazubekommen*
cc	carbon copy	*Verteiler*
CV	curriculum vitae	*Lebenslauf*
DIY	Do-it-Yourself	*Heimwerken*
IT	information technology	*Informationstechnologie*
re.	regarding	*bezüglich*
ref.	reference	*Zeichen (im Brief)*
USP	Unique Selling Proposition / Point	*Alleinstellungsmerkmal Hauptverkaufsargument*
VAT	value added tax	*Mehrwertsteuer, Umsatzsteuer*

Differences in vocabulary

British English	American English	German
a ten pound note	a ten dollar bill	*(Geld)schein*
biscuit	cookie	*Keks*
car park	parking lot	*Parkplatz*
chemists	drugstore	*Drogerie / Apotheke*
chips	French fries	*Pommes / Fritten*
crisps	(potato) chips	*Chips*
fill in a form	fill out a form	*ein Formular ausfüllen*
guarantee	warranty	*Garantie*
ground floor, first floor	first floor, second floor	*Erdgeschoss, 1. Etage*
handbag	purse	*Handtasche*
jam	jelly	*Marmelade*
jelly	jell-o	*Götterspeise*
purse	coin-purse	*Geldbeutel*
lift	elevator	*Aufzug*
mobile (phone)	cell (phone)	*Handy*
Monday to Friday	Monday through (or: thru') Friday	*Montag bis (einschließlich) Freitag*
shop / store	store	*Laden; Geschäft*
shopping trolley	shopping cart	*Einkaufswagen*
sweets	candy	*Süßwaren*
tights	pantyhose	*Strumpfhose*
tin	can	*Dose*
toilet / ladies / gents	restroom	*Toilette*
trainers	sneakers	*Turnschuhe*
trousers	pants	*Hose*
vest	singlet	*Unterhemd*
waistcoat	vest	*Weste*
zip	zipper	*Reißverschluss*

Pronunciation and phonetic symbols

As you know by now, there are no simple rules for spelling in English. Also, the way a word is written does not always show you how to say it.
Dictionaries use special symbols and marks to show how words are pronounced and which syllable has the main stress. In most dictionaries, the symbols are based on a system known as the International Pronunciation Alphabet (IPA).

The letters of the IPA are known as phonetic symbols because they represent sounds. Some are pronounced the way they are written, e.g. [**m**] for **m**oney and [**l**] for **l**ots. Others may not be what you expect, e.g. [**j**] for **y**et and **y**olk, and [**dʒ**] for **j**et and **j**oke.
Below is a list of sounds included in the IPA, with examples of words containing these sounds. Dictionaries usually give a key to symbols, but it is worth learning the basic system anyway.

Consonants

b	(big, back, bubble)
d	(did, dog, daddy)
f	(fall, phone, enough)
g	(go, target, jogging)
h	(hat, house, behind)
j	(yes, onion, vignette)
k	(key, click, chemist)
l	(lot, leg, yellow)
m	(money, some, climb)
n	(no, know, nine)
p	(pig, open, opposite)
r	(red, ring, carry)
s	(see, six, science)
t	(too, two, attraction)
v	(video, van, event)
w	(wet, won, one)
z	(zip, zero, is, easy)
dʒ	(jam, agenda, judge, soldier)
ʃ	(ship, sugar, mission, action)
θ	(three, thick, throat)
ð	(the, that, these)
tʃ	(check, lunch, achieve, nature)
ʒ	(closure, vision, measure, invasion)
ŋ	(sing, long, hang, tongue)

Syllable stress

ˈ	syllable with the main stress e.g. ˈʌndə (<u>un</u>der)
ˌ	syllable with the secondary stress (plus main stress) e.g. ˌʌnˈduː (un<u>do</u>)

Short vowels

ɪ	sit, busy, pocket, women	
e	ten, bed, said	
æ	cat, bad, pattern	
ʌ	run, flood, son, rough	
ɒ	hot, wash, lot	(BE)
ʊ	put, good, should, woman	
ə	the, alone, colour, curious	
i	happy, cosy, funny, pretty	
u	influence, situation, actual	

Long vowels

iː	see, tea, receive, leave	
ɑː	heart, start, arm, park	(BE/AE)
	hot, wash, lot	(AE)
ɔː	saw, floor, north, war	
ɜː	burn, girl, learn, nurse	(BE)
ɜː(r)	burn, girl, learn, nurse	(AE)

Diphthongs

eɪ	day, face, paid, made	
aɪ	sky, high, I'll, aisle	
ɔɪ	boy, coin, choice	
əʊ	go, low, dough	(BE)
oʊ	go, low, grow, dough	(AE)
aʊ	how, house, loud, crowd	
ɪə	near, we're, beer, tier	(BE)
eə	hair, wear, square, care	(BE)
ʊə	sure, rural, jury	
aɪə	buyer, higher, fire, liar	
aʊə	sour, flour, flower	

BE: British English
AE: American English
consonant: Mitlaut / Konsonant, vowel: Selbstlaut / Vokal, diphthong: Doppellaut / Diphthong

Pronunciation and accents

Your **accent** is the way you pronounce words. It can show your regional background (an Australian accent, a Scottish accent) and even your social status (a posh accent, a common accent). **Received pronunciation (RP)** is the regionally neutral accent used by many middle class speakers in England. The American equivalent is known as **General American (GA)**. Some words are pronounced differently in RP and GA, for example:

Examples	**RP**	**GA**
th**ough**t, c**augh**t	[ɔ] as in c**o**re	[ɑː] as in c**a**r
wri**t**er, me**t**al	[t] as in **t**op	[d] as in ri**d**er
d**u**ty, n**ew**	[jʊ] as in b**eau**ty, **you**	[uː] as in m**oo**dy, bl**ue**
hai**r** ca**re**, bea**r**	[eə] silent 'R'	[er] voiced 'R'

Vocabulary

False Friends

ENGLISH	**=**	**GERMAN**	**≠**	**ENGLISH**	**=**	**GERMAN**
current, latest	=	***aktuell***	≠	**actual**	=	*tatsächlich*
cash desk, checkout	=	***Kasse***	≠	**cash**	=	*Bargeld*
advise	=	***beraten***	≠	**berate**	=	*kritisieren*
letter	=	***Brief***	≠	**brief**	=	*kurz*
boss	=	***Chef***	≠	**chef**	=	*Koch (im Restaurant)*
hard-working	=	***engagiert***	≠	**engaged**	=	*verlobt*
label	=	***Etikett***	≠	**etiquette**	=	*Protokoll, Umgangsform*
factory	=	***Fabrik***	≠	**fabric**	=	*Stoff, Gewebe*
personal, friendly	=	***familiär***	≠	**familiar**	=	*vertraut, bekannt*
form	=	***Formular***	≠	**formula**	=	*Formel (mathem.)*
poison	=	***Gift***	≠	**gift**	=	*Geschenk*
mobile phone, cellphone	=	***Handy***	≠	**handy**	=	*nützlich; praktisch*
lend sth. to so.	=	***jm. etw. borgen***	≠	**borrow**	=	*ausleihen*
deposit	=	***Kaution***	≠	**caution**	=	*Vorsicht*
check	=	***kontrollieren***	≠	**control (v.)**	=	*lenken, steuern*
criticism	=	***Kritik***	≠	**critic**	=	*Kritiker*
briefcase / file	=	***Mappe***	≠	**map**	=	*Karte, Stadtplan*

ENGLISH	=	GERMAN	≠	ENGLISH	=	GERMAN
opinion	=	***Meinung***	≠	**meaning**	=	*Bedeutung*
set meal / menu	=	***Menü***	≠	**menu**	=	*Speisekarte*
dung, fertilizer	=	***Mist***	≠	**mist**	=	*leichter Nebel*
(exam) grade, mark	=	***Note***	≠	**note**	=	*Notiz, Anmerkung*
personnel	=	***Personal***	≠	**personal**	=	*persönlich*
brochure, leaflet	=	***Prospekt***	≠	**prospect**	=	*Aussicht, Chance*
commission	=	***Provision***	≠	**provision**	=	*Versorgung, Vorrat*
health-food store	=	***Reformhaus***	≠	**reform house**	=	*Besserungsanstalt*
complaint	=	***Reklamation***	≠	**reclamation**	=	*Landzurückgewinnung*
profitable	=	***rentabel***	≠	**rentable**	=	*vermietbar (Wohnung)*
pension	=	***Rente***	≠	**rent**	=	*Miete*
skirt	=	***Rock***	≠	**rock**	=	*Stein; Fels*
sensitive	=	***sensibel***	≠	**sensible**	=	*vernünftig*
save	=	***sparen***	≠	**spare**	=	*Zusatz- / zusätzlich*
donate (to)	=	***spenden***	≠	**spend**	=	*(Geld / Zeit) ausgeben*
likeable, friendly	=	***sympatisch***	≠	**sympathetic**	=	*mitfühlend*
overview	=	***Übersicht***	≠	**oversight**	=	*Versehen*
entrepreneur	=	***Unternehmer***	≠	**undertaker**	=	*Leichenbestatter*
department store	=	***Warenhaus***	≠	**warehouse**	=	*Lager*
preserve	=	***konservieren***	≠	**conserve**	=	*sparen*
loan	=	***Kredit***	≠	**credit**	=	*Gutschrift, Guthaben*
spicy, hot	=	***scharf***	≠	**sharp**	=	*spitz, scharf (Gegenstände)*
posh, elegant, upscale	=	***nobel***	≠	**noble**	=	*edelmutig, adelig*

ENGLISH	=	GERMAN	≠	ENGLISH	=	GERMAN
instalment	=	***Rate***	≠	**rate**	=	*Satz, Kurs (z. B. Zinssatz), Wechselkurs*
bulletin board, notice board	=	***Schwarzes Brett***	≠	**blackboard**	=	*Tafel (im Klassen-zimmer)*
insurance policy	=	***Police***	≠	**police**	=	*Polizei*

Vocabulary fields

People in retailing
supervisor
supervise, to
colleague
co-worker (AE)
member of staff
staff member
trainee
manager
head of department
sales assistant

Activities in retailing
make a sale, to
sell, to
buy, to
offer, to
serve, to
complain, to
deal with a complaint, to
self-service
train, to
training, to do
responsible for, to be
in charge of, to be
report to, to
duty
task
responsibility

Types of retail outlet
branch
department store
supermarket
kiosk
market stall
factory outlet
shopping mall
shopping centre
speciality shop
specialty store (AE)
shop (BE)
store (AE)
vending machine

Reputation and quality
to be of superior quality
to have a (good) reputation for …
to stand for good quality
to be the market leader in …

Style and fashion
to be stylish / fashionable / trendy
to be traditional / classic
to have an attractive design
to be 'in' / to be the latest

Technology and use
to be (highly) sophisticated
to be state-of-the-art
to be well-made / -built / -constructed
to be reliable / robust / durable
to be efficient / economical
to be user-friendly / easy-to-use
to be versatile / have many uses
to offer convenience / comfort
to be convenient / useful / handy

Fabrics, materials, metals
suede
leather
cotton
wool
polyester
nylon
silk
fur
wood
aluminium
gold
silver
bronze

Advertising and promotion
poster
leaflet
advertise, to
advertisement
advertising
to promote
promotion
to offer
special offer
buy two, get one free
two for the price of one

Price
a two-euro coin
cash discount
including / excluding VAT
quantity discount
ten-pound note / ten-dollar bill
to afford a product
to be 20% off
to be a bargain
to be overpriced
to be reasonably priced
to borrow money from someone
to change a currency
to charge someone for something
to deposit money in(to) an account
to donate money (n. donation)
to earn money
to grant / give a discount
to have money in an account
to invest money in something
to invoice someone for something
to issue a receipt
to lend money to someone
to lose money
to offer (excellent) value for money
to owe money
to pay a bill / an invoice
to pay a charge
to pay a lump sum
to pay by cheque / credit card
to pay for (+ the thing bought)
to pay in cash
to pay in instalments
to pay interest on a loan
to pay within ten days
to run out of money
to save money
to sell at a competitive price
to spend money
to steal money
to transfer a sum from one account to another
to waste money
to win money
to withdraw money from an account
total amount
unit price

Irregular verbs

infinitive	past simple	past participle	German
to **be**	**was / were**	**been**	*sein*
to **beat**	**beat**	**beaten**	*besiegen, schlagen*
to **become**	**became**	**become**	*werden*
to **begin**	**began**	**begun**	*beginnen*
to **bend**	**bent**	**bent**	*beugen*
to **bite**	**bit**	**bitten**	*beißen*
to **blow**	**blew**	**blown**	*blasen*
to **break**	**broke**	**broken**	*brechen*
to **bring**	**brought**	**brought**	*bringen*
to **build**	**built**	**built**	*bauen*
to **burst**	**burst**	**burst**	*platzen*
to **buy**	**bought**	**bought**	*kaufen*
to **catch**	**caught**	**caught**	*fangen*
to **choose**	**chose**	**chosen**	*wählen*

infinitive	past simple	past participle	German
to **come**	**came**	**come**	*kommen*
to **cost**	**cost**	**cost**	*kosten*
to **cut**	**cut**	**cut**	*schneiden*
to **deal (with)**	**dealt**	**dealt**	*be(handeln)*
to **draw**	**drew**	**drawn**	*zeichnen*
to **dream**	**dreamed / dreamt**	**dreamed / dreamt**	*träumen*
to **drink**	**drank**	**drunk**	*trinken*
to **drive**	**drove**	**driven**	*fahren*
to **eat**	**ate**	**eaten**	*essen*
to **fall**	**fell**	**fallen**	*fallen*
to **feed**	**fed**	**fed**	*füttern*
to **feel**	**felt**	**felt**	*(sich) fühlen*
to **fight**	**fought**	**fought**	*kämpfen*
to **find**	**found**	**found**	*finden*
to **fly**	**flew**	**flown**	*fliegen*
to **forget**	**forgot**	**forgotten**	*vergessen*
to **freeze**	**froze**	**frozen**	*gefrieren, frieren*
to **get**	**got**	**got**	*holen, bekommen*
to **give**	**gave**	**given**	*geben*
to **go**	**went**	**gone**	*gehen*
to **grown**	**grew**	**grown**	*wachsen, (an)bauen*
to **hang**	**hung**	**hung**	*hängen*
to **have**	**had**	**had**	*haben*
to **hear**	**heard**	**heard**	*hören*
to **hide**	**hid**	**hidden**	*(sich) verstecken*
to **hit**	**hit**	**hit**	*schlagen*
to **hold**	**held**	**held**	*halten*
to **hurt**	**hurt**	**hurt**	*verletzen, wehtun*
to **keep**	**kept**	**kept**	*(be)halten*
to **know**	**knew**	**known**	*wissen, kennen*
to **lead**	**led**	**lead**	*führen*
to **learn**	**learned/learnt**	**learned/learnt**	*beugen*
to **leave**	**left**	**left**	*(ver)lassen*
to **lend**	**lent**	**lent**	*(ver)leihen*
to **let**	**let**	**let**	*lassen*
to **lie**	**lay**	**lain**	*liegen*

infinitive	past simple	past participle	German
to **light**	**lit**	**lit**	*beleuchten, anzünden*
to **lose**	**lost**	**lost**	*verlieren*
to **make**	**made**	**made**	*machen, tun*
to **mean**	**meant**	**meant**	*bedeuten, meinen*
to **meet**	**met**	**met**	*treffen, begegnen*
to **pay**	**paid**	**paid**	*bezahlen*
to **put**	**put**	**put**	*setzen, stellen, legen*
to **read**	**read**	**read**	*lesen*
to **rewind**	**rewound**	**rewound**	*zurückspülen*
to **ride**	**rode**	**ridden**	*reiten, fahren*
to **ring**	**rang**	**rung**	*klingeln, anrufen*
to **rise**	**rose**	**risen**	*sich erheben, steigen*
to **run**	**ran**	**run**	*laufen, rennen*
to **say**	**said**	**said**	*sagen*
to **see**	**saw**	**seen**	*sehen*
to **sell**	**sold**	**sold**	*verkaufen*
to **send**	**sent**	**sent**	*schicken, senden*
to **set**	**set**	**set**	*setzen, stellen, legen*
to **sew**	**sewed**	**sewed/sewn**	*nähen*
to **shake**	**shook**	**shaken**	*schütteln*
to **shine**	**shone**	**shone**	*scheinen*
to **shoot**	**shot**	**shot**	*schießen*
to **show**	**showed**	**shown**	*zeigen*
to **shrink**	**shrank**	**shrunk**	*einlaufen, eingehen (Stoff)*
to **shut**	**shut**	**shut**	*schließen*
to **sing**	**sang**	**sung**	*singen*
to **sink**	**sank**	**sunk**	*sinken*
to **sit**	**sat**	**sat**	*sitzen*
to **sleep**	**slept**	**slept**	*schlafen*
to **slide**	**slid**	**slid**	*rutschen*
to **smell**	**smelled/smelt**	**smelled/smelt**	*riechen*
to **speak**	**spoke**	**spoken**	*sprechen*
to **spell**	**spelled/spelt**	**spelled/spelt**	*buchstabieren*
to **spend**	**spent**	**spent**	*ausgeben (Geld), verbringen (Zeit)*
to **spill**	**spilled/spilt**	**spilled/spilt**	*ausschütten, vergießen*

infinitive	past simple	past participle	German
to **split**	**split**	**split**	*spalten*
to **stand**	**stood**	**stood**	*stehen*
to **steal**	**stole**	**stolen**	*stehlen*
to **stick**	**stuck**	**stuck**	*kleben, stecken*
to **swell**	**swelled**	**swollen**	*anschwellen*
to **swim**	**swam**	**swum**	*schwimmen*
to **take**	**took**	**taken**	*nehmen, (hin)bringen*
to **teach**	**taught**	**taught**	*lehren, unterrichten*
to **tear**	**tore**	**torn**	*(zer)reißen*
to **tell**	**told**	**told**	*erzählen, sagen*
to **think**	**thought**	**thought**	*denken*
to **throw**	**threw**	**thrown**	*werfen*
to **understand**	**understood**	**understood**	*verstehen*
to **wake**	**woke**	**woken**	*wecken, aufwachen*
to **wear**	**wore**	**worn**	*tragen (Kleidung)*
to **win**	**won**	**won**	*gewinnen*
to **wind**	**wound**	**wound**	*sich schlängeln*
to **write**	**wrote**	**written**	*schreiben*

Bildquellenverzeichnis

Adidas AG: S. 23

Apple: S. 23

Steffi Becker: S. 13, 16, 21, 23, 31, 59, 60, 104, 108

Bildungsverlag EINS: S. 8, 17, 27, 49, 52, 61, 91, 94, 100, 115, 124

BMW AG: S. 23

Deutsche Postbank AG: S. 23, 35

Fotolia: S. 7 (Peter Niehold), 9 (Pavel Losevsky), 10 (Irina Fischer), 10 (Exquisine), 10 (chiyachat), 10 (Purdythings), 10 (David Hernandez), 10 (Silence), 18 (gajatz), 18 (Stephen Coburn), 25 (elemental imaging), 30 (photoGrapHie), 32 (Marc Rigaud), 36 (Leonid Nyshko), 36 (Ozgur Aydin), 36 (Sebastian Kaulitzki), 36 (chiyachat), 36 (Svetlana Gladkova), 39 (Kurhan), 53 (overthehill), 54 (bilderbox), 55 (Georgios Kollidas), 58 (auris), 69 (Rtimages), 71 (Timon Romeijn), 72 (Carl Keyes), 72 (fürstin), 75 (Elke Dennis), 76 (tragidi), 79 (Tom Mc Nemar), 82 (Andres Rodriguez), 82 (Alx), 83 (Yuri Arcurs), 84 (schweitzer-degen), 84 (Wladimir Wetzel), 84 (Zauberhut), 84 (Baloncic), 84 (Timo Schwach), 84 (Klaus Sailer), 90 (photlook), 90 (Oxymoron), 91 (Dron), 91 (massi b), 92 (Andrey Armyagov), 94 (pmphoto), 96 (cilin), 96 (Klaus Eppele), 96 (Alx), 98 (Franck Boston), 98 (Darren Baker), 99 (Artmann Witte), 102 (Cmon), 105 (amaxim), 113 (Franz Pfluegl), 115 (Palabra), 124 (Oxymoron), 124 (Hans-Joachim Roy), 124 (Christian Pauschert), 124 (O'Jay Barbee), 124 (CD-Fotografik), 124 (Tino Baab), 124 (Daniel Käsler), 124 (Mirko Meier), 124 (Aleksander Potapov), 128 (FX Berlin), 128 (Svetlana Gladkova), 149 (FX Berlin), 149 (chiyachat)

H&M: S. 23

MEV: S. 10, 22, 24, 25, 30, 32, 36, 37, 38, 42, 54, 55, 58, 67, 72, 73, 82, 84, 85, 86, 87, 90, 91, 92, 96, 96, 100, 102, 104, 105, 110, 114, 115, 116, 119, 120, 122, 124, 149

Project Photo: s. 10, 30, 72, 76, 115

Vodafone D2 GmbH: S. 35

Oliver Wetterauer: S. 66